Endorsements

Through this whole experience, capturing stories has been crucial. What we have been through is intergenerational and it is through the telling of stories that we can all begin to heal. Each telling releases us from being stuck in trauma, leads people out, looking forward into the future. *When The Smoke Clears* gives us lessons to take away and prompts us to have those important conversations. It reminds us, just as the black trees are shooting green leaves, we too are branching out and healing.

Mayor Liz Innes, Eurobodalla Shire, NSW, Australia.

I'm so glad Chrissy put this book together. It is important that what happened is documented. *When The Smoke Clears* is significant in that it gets the story out about volunteers and people directly affected by the fires. This is a narrative of hope. Our community has come together as one, stronger than ever before. People are helping people—conscious now of what really matters. It is great to be given this opportunity to share our story. What better person to tell it than Chrissy, straight from the heart using first-hand accounts.

Captain Ian Aitken, Batemans Bay Rural Fire Services

At a time of incredible difficulty, extraordinary storyteller Chrissy Guinery provides great encouragement through her book *When The Smoke Clears*. Within these pages Chrissy brings timely inspiration; assuring us of our ability to stand firm and rely on God to get us through any crisis. Psalm 91 is brought to light—a timely reminder of faith over fear. This is a compelling read!

**Ruth Swift, Acts Global Churches
National Leadership Team**

WHEN THE SMOKE SMOKE *Clears*

CHRISSY GUINERY is all about empowering others. As a successful author and motivational speaker, Chrissy is renowned for her infectious joy, passionate faith and her desire to see others rise to fulfil their purpose and potential. To achieve this, she has been sharing her life secrets for more than 20 years in a down-to-earth relatable style, leaving people with essential tools for pursuing a more effective and fulfilling life. She is the author of *Falling Up Stairs* (2016) and *Room to Breathe* (2018).

Dedication

To Harper, London and Lennox
and Mum and to the
One who created me to shine

CHRISSY GUINERY

WHEN THE SMOKE Clears

Surviving the Australian bushfires

A Fifty Days Press book

Published by
Fifty Days Press
Sydney Australia
fiftydays.com.au
© Chrissy Guinery 2020
First published 2020

10 9 8 7 6 5 4 3

ISBN: 978-0-6487934-2-7 (paperback)
        978-0-6487934-3-4 (kindle)
        978-0-6487934-4-1 (ePub)

A catalogue record for this book is available from the National Library of Australia

Design *SD creative*
Cover image *Step Guinery*
Editor *Peter Hallett*
Printer *SOS Print + Media*

The author acknowledges the invaluable contributions of Dr Rob Gordon, Mayor Liz Innes, RFS Captain Ian Aitken, Ps Garren Walton, Lauren Edwards, Cassia Walton, Kelita Bourke, Jordan Innes, Julie Steedman, Donna Hunter, Jim Hughes, James and the girlfriends Messenger group who have allowed their written and spoken stories of surviving the Australian bushfires to be included in *When The Smoke Clears*.

Fifty Days Press
BOOKS THAT BREATHE LIFE

Contents

'My grandson climbs up onto my lap and looks up at me. He tells me, "The fire is a baddie. It's big and mean and I want to punch it and knock it down."'

CHAPTER 1

Their home is gone

From the fireground—December 31, 2019

My middle-daughter's house is burning down and I've lost contact with my eldest daughter as the fire front threatens her home. It's the last day of 2019 and feels like end of the world.

I'm bawling now. I don't want my daughter's house to be burned to the ground. I'm desperate to hear from my eldest daughter, caught in the fire further south, out of contact, out there—somewhere. Is she safe? Were they able to get out in time?

My mumma-heart is grieving, I long to gather my chickens and snuggle them all close and safe. I want to turn back time. I want to change this crazy day. I want to run. I want to hide. I want to hold my grandchildren. I want to hug my daughters. I want to cry and I want to scream. I'm desperate to see these family members, but I don't want to leave the ones I'm with.

I have five children with partners and all of them have children of their own. Four of these families are surrounded by fires. That means 11 of my 14 grandchildren are somewhere amidst this chaos! Our son Caleb was down visiting from the Gold Coast and left a couple of days ago. I thank God that he and wife Tess and three daughters Peaches, Hopps and Junee are out of harm's way. They were amazed by the amount of smoke and haze everywhere. Most of the time we try to ignore it, (it has kind of become our 'norm'), but truth be told, we are sick of living like '40-a-day' smokers. Since mid-October we have been breathing smoke, and that, combined with constant stress and anxiety, is making us all feel so tired.

And now this. Now the unthinkable.

I feel like I've failed my family because I couldn't keep them safe and protect them. I feel failure creeping up the back of my neck. I know it's a lie, but it doesn't stop the feelings, the overwhelming emotions, the grief. It frightens me to think how quickly our world can unravel.

I want my family to be with me, to all be together—all my children and their families—so I can take them somewhere safe from all of this. But where? There is nowhere to run. Nobody knows where safety is. Everything is burning. We are blocked on every side. The Princes Highway north and south is closed. The Kings Highway to the west is closed. We're trapped!

I have to get to Kelita, my middle daughter who has just lost everything. I need to hug her, to comfort her, to help her process this tragedy. How could this happen to our family? I desperately want to make everything right, but how can I? It isn't right. It's so wrong. No young family should lose their home and everything they own in one fell swoop.

It is a cruel waiting game, and I'm torn. I want my family to be with me; to be together. And then, in an instant, I also desperately want to go somewhere by myself and sort this mess out with God. I want to know how and why this happened—to us? I think of all the Scriptures stored up in my heart. I know I can trust Him and rely upon His unconditional love and faithfulness. For more than 40 years I have made a habit of doing just that, and He has never let me down. My heart reassures me that it's okay, but my mind is all over the shop. Where is my eldest daughter and her family? 'Have you got them God? Please look after them and keep them safe,' I plead.

I need a little time out. I jump in the shower, turn on the taps, and cold water hits me like a slap in the face. There's no hot water because there's no power. The petrol generator in the shed drives the pump for the water, but the gas heater needs electricity to spark it into life. I don't mind. I don't need to be comfortable. Being comfortable somehow seems wrong in these circumstances. How can I be comfortable when one of my daughters is out there somewhere trying to escape the fires while another daughter and her family have no home to go back to?

I bury my head under the cold spray and I cry. I let the tears flow. It's a safe space and I need to let things out. Once I start, it's *open the flood gates*. I double over and get lost in big, hard, full-on sobs. It's not controlled and is not pretty. Not even under the flow of the cold water can I pretend to be okay. I don't want to get out looking puffy-eyed and snotty-nosed but I've got no choice. After too many minutes, I realise I have to get out and stop wasting precious water. We're in a drought and haven't seen rain for months. I want to curl up and spend more time feeling sorry for myself, but I can't. I have things to do and people to care for. 'Get your act together girl,' I tell myself. And I do— well at least for the moment.

Hubby, Step, recognises 'that face', of course he does, we've been together for 42 years. He knows how upset I am and wraps his arms around me the moment I emerge from my bathroom refuge. We hug and cry together. We're going to get through this, we assure one another wordlessly. We're going to stand together. We're going to stand on our faith. We've made it through some tough times and we'll make it through this. But the enormity of what we're going through, reeling from, trapped within, is too much to carry. Too much to hold in. Later, we'll be brave for the family, we know we will. We'll be their rock... after we cry together in this unguarded moment. Though words may fail us, our hearts don't. Our faith does not fail us. Our hope will not fail us. We'll weep in one another's arms because that's what married folk do in the midst of crisis.

Once dressed, tears and snot in check, I busy myself. I can't sit back and do nothing, and neither can Step. We have so much adrenaline and nervous energy coursing through our veins, we have to stay busy—or else. I can't be dwelling on my fears about my eldest daughter or that my middle daughter's home is now a pile of rubble and ash. I scramble around, picking things up and putting them down again. Step continues to prepare the property so that if the fire does threaten our 'Long Beach Love Shack', which the doomsayers are certain will happen, we might have a chance of saving it. As we hear reports of hundreds of homes lost up and down the coast, the likelihood of our place in the bush surviving seems slim indeed. In spite of this, we choose to be optimistic about believing for a good outcome.

I have a trained mind. Forty years of walking with God and discovering the Father's heart, has instilled in me a confidence in the power of prayer. I talk with Him all through the day and night. I feel His presence as strongly as I felt Step's arms around me earlier. He has protected us in the past and He will protect us in the future. He knows our every need and He promises to hold us and support us through it all. Together, we will get through. He comforts us so that we can go and share the same comfort with those in need. He makes us strong so that we can be 'a shoulder to cry on' for those that are hurting. He calls us to be his hands, His feet, His mouthpiece, but most of all He wants us to reveal His heart to those that don't know Him.

A difficult night passes and finally we are able to venture out to try and find our daughter. We drive slowly and cautiously, with headlights on, through thick smoke, past roadblocks and burning buildings, and through deserted streets that are normally spilling over with tourists and holiday-makers. The air is thick, the stench is putrid—almost unbearable with so many homes, shops and businesses burning around us and belching out plumes of toxic smoke. Not surprisingly, more and more people are wearing facemasks to protect themselves, but I can't help but think their efforts are probably futile. Every second person has had sore eyes and an irritating cough for weeks and now my nose won't stop running.

And then I see Kelita, with her oldest son.

Finally, we've found them! As we jump out of the car to run to them, my throat tightens as I try to keep myself together. I give her a big mumma-hug, before turning my attention to grandson Harper, who gets called 'H'. I squeeze him tight and don't want to let him go—this boy who has endured so much.

'My house burnt down, Granny,' he says without emotion.

The poor little fella! He is six-years-old. We walk to find Kelita's husband and the other two kids and we give them their share of hugs and kisses. Step, my 81-year-old Mum, my daughter, her hubby, their three children and I, head to where they are staying for now, grab a cuppa, and settle in to hear about their ordeal.

I nurse one-year-old Lennox, while he messily consumes a nectarine, dripping juice onto my tights. I hug three-year-old London. And then I am riveted as their story unfolds of evacuation and being trapped and fires bursting alight in front of them. They tell of how they received news of their home burning and how Kelita's brother-in-law was attempting to save it. News that it was too late. News that their home had gone.

They share with us about heading back toward their home through what seemed like a warzone, with fires taking down tall trees on both sides of the road, witnessing other people's houses alight. We're gripping our seats as her hubby tells of rushing up to Catalina just in time to see the last of the flames engulf what was once his family's home. He had taken his mobile phone out and filmed his home's final end, flames leaping from every shattered window, the top story already just rubble on the ground.

We gather around his phone and watch the short video together, speechless. It comes to an abrupt end. Our minds can't fathom it. And we play it again. It is incomprehensible. Nothing seems real. My grandson climbs up onto my lap and looks up at me. He tells me, 'The fire is a baddie. It's big and mean and I want to punch it and knock it down.'

Don't we all, mate, don't we all.

I've brought some clothes for each of the kids from my youngest daughter, who has five children of her own. Her kids also raided their toy boxes and H receives the red motorbike his cousin Hayz has generously chosen for him. I leave him sitting on my lap as the adults talk over his head. He drives his motorbike on the table, backward and forwards, props it up on its stand, picks it up, drives it again, turns it over, spins the wheels, and drives it some more. The motorbike, this priceless gift from his cousin, means the world to him.

He looks up at me after half an hour and says, 'I have one toy now Granny'. I swallow hard and fight back the tears. My heart breaks into a million pieces.

CHAPTER 2
Firestorms

Things were never looking good, but we had no idea that they would look so bad! The Aussie bushfire season officially begins on October 1, but by September of 2019, fires were already burning in many drought-affected areas in both Queensland and NSW. A decade of dry conditions and years of drought were taking their toll; combustible fuel lay in wait almost everywhere. By early October there was also a large fire south-east of Broome in Western Australia that destroyed around 870,00 hectares (2.2 million acres).

Here on the South Coast of NSW, fires were also burning in a number of locations as early as November, heralding the calamitous summer we were soon to experience. Who would have known that these fires, while problematic, were not as serious a threat to communities as the summer fires that would soon follow? Of course at the time, the impact of these fires was dismissed lightly, but the ongoing inconvenience for people through regular closure of roads and highways was just the beginning of us becoming completely hemmed-in. With heavy smoke blanketing the South Coast for weeks on end, the simple act of breathing became a challenge—causing a widespread increase in fear and anxiety among our community and many others.

Living under threat

When our hometown of Batemans Bay hit the news with the potential of more fires, the pressure was turned-up a notch or two. Suddenly it was frightfully close to home and all the more real. We may have empathy for those who are affected in other places, but the moment you and yours are threatened, everything takes on new meaning. Everything is magnified! Suddenly this story is about you, it is about your loved-ones, and it is not a story in which you were ever hoping to feature.

At the same time as Batemans Bay was in the firing-line (literally), there were fires breaking out further down the NSW coast and right across eastern Victoria in the Gippsland region. A series of fires in early-to-mid December also devastated 210,000 hectares of Kangaroo Island in South Australia. We, likewise, had reports of fires raging through north-eastern Tasmania and some of the wilderness areas to the south, as temperatures soared into the forties. At one point it seemed like most of the nation was alight; firefighters battling bushfires everywhere.

Two large fires, the Currowan Fire to the north, and the Clyde Mountain Fire to the west of Batemans Bay, were the biggest concern for us, and with catastrophic weather conditions predicted, it felt like we were facing an unwinnable fight, with our family right in the thick of it. People began to get anxious. Suddenly, we couldn't get enough information about fires. They began to feature predominantly in every conversation—a preoccupation which was very new to us, but would become second nature.

Though severe fire warnings were an everyday occurrence, it was still difficult to imagine how a major fire could seriously threaten a coastal oasis like Batemans Bay, where the average rainfall usually provided a reliable safeguard. We'd always been a safe space before. Owing to the fact that most of us have relatively short memories, bushfires were only thought to be a risk for places 'out west' or across the notorious fire corridor of Victoria.

Surely authorities were making a mountain out of a molehill so that we wouldn't become complacent. We were right on the coast, 'girt by sea', for heaven's sake. It seemed inevitable that we would be okay and the much overdue rain would soon put an end to these destructive fires.

From mid-October, throughout November and into early December, we were on high alert, with my youngest daughter, Jordan, her hubby Mace and their five kids evacuated twice. This was a precautionary measure against the Currowan Fire. Sparked by lightning, it was out of control and burning to the north of Batemans Bay, threatening costal townships like Depot Beach, South Durras and Long Beach. It had grown to 2,500 hectares within the first day and was to go on, spreading in all directions, destroying hundreds of properties and nearly half a million hectares (over a million acres) of land.

By the time of Jordan's second evacuation to a downstairs area at a beachside home at Surfside, they were already growing tired of waiting and not knowing if or when the fires would strike. Their precious belongings, things they had only recently purchased, like their new lounge and bedroom suite, had been loaded onto a borrowed truck. Their cars had been filled with all they could gather and they were roughly 'camped out' in a small space. The novelty wore off quickly. Things were to get even more precarious when the weary evacuees were *again* evacuated from this 'safe space' just days after arriving for the second time.

All around, people were exhausted by the continuous uncertainty and disruption to everyday life. Do we stay or do we go? Are the fires heading this way or have they turned? Are the fires under control or are we still under threat? This didn't just require daily decision-making; it often demanded our attention hourly as each new report filtered in. I even overheard some people say that they would rather the fire burn everything quickly than have to play this perpetual waiting game. In the wake of what has happened to our beautiful towns, they would be thinking differently now.

Temperatures continued to climb and the winds were unpredictable and blowing from the dreaded north-west. With still no rain on the horizon, fire crews were stretched beyond limit and struggling to contain any of the larger fires. Once more fires began to break out seemingly everywhere. There was little that could be done apart from getting to safety and staying out of the path of the fire. At the same time, Australian towns and cities recorded the worst air quality in the world, with the nation's capital, Canberra, all but shutting down due to the smoke. We needed rain—a week of good, solid, soaking rain. Nothing else would do. Even those without faith were turning to God and asking for a downpour.

An unfamiliar Christmas

Jordan and her family reluctantly returned to their home as December took on a strange and unfamiliar rhythm leading up to Christmas. A week before Christmas Day, we did our best to put the fires out of our minds and to resume some sort of normality. We were tired of the warnings of impending disaster, and so we did what people do best—we allowed complacency and denial to creep in. This, I have discovered, is quite a normal phenomenon when people are under constant threat. It may not be logical or practical, but it does provide a temporary reprieve, at least within our minds. We're only able to be under constant stress for so long before we find a method to relieve the tension.

I have to say though, looking back, we truly didn't think the fires would get to us. We were well aware of the diligence of our local Rural Fire Service (RFS) brigade and this helped create a sense of safety, despite what we were seeing on news reports. Though the media was portraying a horror story and warning visitors and holiday-makers to stay well away, we had been living under smoke-filled skies and on alert for so long (and with nothing too serious happening), that we just wanted to get on with life and put it aside for a while.

We knew that Christmas holiday season was going to be much quieter than usual, and that the local economy would struggle as a result, but even so, we attempted to put our energy into celebrating. With the King's Highway closed to Canberra (halting its annual horde of holiday visitors) and predictions it would remain closed for at least a month, we focused on our Christmas preparations. The shopping centres were eerily quiet, not the usual chaos and rushing and pushing and carpark road-rage that normally came with the 'silly season'. Shopping was a pleasure, consumerism and commercialism didn't really affect the way we purchased. We gathered foods, drinks and gifts with order and an unusual common-sense that is not normally present at this time of year.

Soon it was time for the annual Christmas Carols event, but because of recent fires to the north and west of town, the sports ground where it was scheduled to be held, was being used as temporary accommodation for evacuees. The fire situation eased-off just enough for the decision to go ahead and hold the carols. With a scaled-down version of our usual community celebrations, we gathered nevertheless. In the midst of pending calamity, no one was completely sure how much celebrating the community would be up for, and so the evening was much smaller and more intimate than usual. Our sound systems and stage set-up were unable to arrive, as they were coming from Canberra, and that road was still closed. A makeshift stage and a few microphones were offered, and we made do.

I remember sitting on our colourful picnic rug, singing along to *Silent Night* and thinking about the grand scale of this community evening in past years. Yet this night, with people huddling and singing quietly together, it seemed more real and so much more in line with what I imagine Christmas to be about. Nobody was talking about gifts and all the *stuff* they had to buy, and the usual madness and consumerism seemed to be way down the priority list. Nobody was complaining about how the night could have been run better, because we were all so appreciative of some time out, where we weren't thinking, talking and stressing about fires. The atmosphere was beautiful, with a real sense of a community pulling together. I was proud of our churches, bringing this beautiful reprieve for our community.

Instead of the usual selection of foods and activities on the fair ground, the night ran simply. Grab your tickets from the cheery volunteers in front of the canteen and cash them in for drinks, sausage sandwiches, and Lion's Club donuts. Everything was free. Imagine that! A huge community event with free food, drinks and rides! Incredible. It felt old-fashioned, with that neighbourly sort of vibe I remember as a kid growing up in the 1970s, back when things were simple and everything didn't have to involve flashing lights, production, dancers, a show and every other fandangle thing to keep us entertained, or we were complaining we didn't get our money's worth. You know what I mean?

Just days before the event there had been evacuees in cars and tents and vans filling the very grounds where we spread our coloured rugs and camp chairs and now we were all so relieved to be there, together, safe, at least for this one night.

As we headed home afterwards, a convoy of cars filled with happy souls, most of us returning to homes without power, you could feel that familiar and comforting Christmas spirit in the air. We were reminded of God's love and commitment to us all, seen in the message of Christmas, so that even in our suffering we could take heart in knowing that we are never alone or abandoned. For such a simple, grassroots, back-to-basics Christmas get-together, it is one that I will fondly remember for years to come.

Days later we were celebrating Christmas with the whole family at my eldest daughter's home at Mossy Point where we shared gifts, told stories, played games, swam in the pool, and of course, ate and drank more than we needed. My 81-year-old Mum had travelled down to celebrate Christmas with the 26 of us: Step and I, our five children and their partners, and our 14 grandchildren. Things were going to be fine. The fires would soon be a bad memory and the town would recover—eventually. No worries! I'm sure you're familiar with this type of wishful thinking or rationalisation.

A dangerous year's end

My optimism was short-lived, as the last days of the year approached and there was no reprieve from the dangerously hot, dry conditions. Concern over the weather predictions for New Year's Eve reached new heights, with the word of choice being 'catastrophic' to emphasise the severity of our situation. Fireworks displays were being cancelled all across the state, and there was heated debate about whether the famous Sydney New Year's Eve fireworks should go ahead—it felt like they were thumbing-their noses at those of us in bushfire zones, where there was panic if someone was to even strike a match!

The first State of Emergency due to the bushfires was implemented for a week on November 11, the first time there had been one in NSW since 2013. This was followed by a second on December 19, with the NSW Fire Commissioner advising people close to fires, such as us, to evacuate and to think twice about staying to defend their homes. The main point emphasised was to make the decision early and to be properly prepared. Even RFS veterans were surprised and intimidated by the ferocity and unpredictability of this season's fires. And yet, up to this point, even though fires along the South Coast had destroyed hundreds of thousands of hectares of forest and national parks, and were still categorised as being 'out-of-control', private properties and homes had been mostly spared. No one could have imagined how much and how quickly this would change during the next 24 hours as the monster was to tear through the Eurobodalla Shire!

From the fireground—December 31, 2019

It's New Year's Eve and we wake to a hot, stifling day, with temperatures quickly climbing into the 30s and beyond. It isn't long before the sickly-hot nor-wester begins to blow causing everything in its path to sag and wilt. From the get-go it is obvious we are in for it! The first radio reports of the day confirm that the Clyde Mountain Fire has spread to the south-west of Batemans Bay to a little place called Runnyford. From there other fires are being driven south towards the local tourist mecca called Mogo Wildlife Park.

As conditions worsen the question of evacuation is one we must address. Previous evacuations amounted to little more than an inconvenient fire drill, so we cling to our hope that this will be another false alarm. We discuss various versions of our fire plan for the property and we keep swinging from stay and defend to evacuate early. Step, Mum and I talk about staying at the Long Beach property in our little Love Shack to try and defend it. If things get too hot and we are losing the battle, we plan to jump in the swimming pool, blankets on the ready to put over our heads to survive.

Eventually we settle the question, we feel equipped to stay—this time.

As more news reports come in, we hear that Mogo has been devastated and that everything is gone. We later discover that this is not completely correct and that while more than half the shops and many homes have been destroyed, including Old Mogo Town, some are spared, as is the famous Mogo Wildlife Park, thanks to the incredible courage of management and staff. Still, our tears flow freely with the sense of loss for Mogo residents and the people of the Eurobodalla. A little later we hear that many more homes in Malua Bay, Rosedale, Surf Beach, and Dunn's Creek Road have been razed. I keep thinking, 'How can this be happening to us here in our coastal paradise?'

On hearing about the fire's path through Malua Bay, we wonder about our beautiful friend James, who lives in a rural setting with lots of bush around his property. We try to call him but all the phone networks are down. This only adds to the apocalyptic sense that anything could happen and that we may not know about it until it's too late. We try a video call on Messenger. Somehow in the midst of all this mayhem we connect with our friend. He's fighting the tail-end of the fire front that hit his place. Still charged with adrenaline, he's hooting and hollering and fist-pumping the air because the fire has passed and even though his sheds, fences and garden are gone, his house is still standing—with a huge hole in the roof and a flood of water poured into his loungeroom to save it.

Using his mobile phone, he pans around his property revealing the devastation the fire has wrought. He had dozens of fruit trees, now reduced to smouldering black stumps of charcoal. He tells us how he almost didn't make it, when he nearly succumbed to the fire as it sucked the oxygen out of the air. Shocked, but thankful to be alive, he says that, given the choice, he would never do it again.

An hour or two later, we hear that a number of spot fires have sprung up in Catalina, which is where our middle daughter's home is. We desperately try to track the position of these fires with the 'Fires Near Me' app, but it's difficult to see exactly where they are. Our worst fears are confirmed when we see and read that the fire front is directly behind our daughter's place in a dry gully, full of overgrown bush, sticks and leaf litter. Only two days before, we were there to collect the last of our belongings, that we had been storing under their house. As we were leaving, Step was shaking his head and mumbling about the impossibility of defending such a place should a fire come through. Little did we know that it would soon be engulfed by flames and destroyed.

When our poor local firies, who at this stage are stretched way beyond their limits, do manage to get to the home, all they can do is make a quick assessment, knowing it is too late to save anything. They quickly move on to try and save the next home.

My daughter's home is a smoky tumble of bricks, edged with curls of corrugated iron. Everything they own is gone.

'Somehow in the midst of all this mayhem we connect with our friend. He's fighting the tail-end of the fire front that hit his place. Still charged with adrenaline, he's hooting and hollering and fist-pumping the air because the fire has passed...'

CHAPTER 3
Finding a safe place

Many moons ago, one of my girlfriends from church set up a 'Friends' chat page on Messenger. I call us *girlfriends*, but I think the youngest of us is 58-years-old and the oldest 84. There's just the six of us on this friends chat: Susan, Robin, Sylvia, Pam, Elsie and I. We have each other's backs through the everyday challenges of life as wives or widows, single or married, mums, friends and 'Soul Sisters', as we like to call ourselves.

With their permission, conversations and thoughts from some of these 'chats' are included throughout *When The Smoke Clears*, as a way of bringing you into the personal realties of surviving the Australian bushfires. Somehow, the six of us together have been able to maintain and grow our faith in the midst of the mayhem of the fires and are finding combined strength in our recovery journeys. I believe there is a certain potency in having people around you with whom you can share your concerns and feelings, and when these people stand by you and take the time to pray for you, it provides great support through trauma, making for a speedier healing and a less-bumpy recovery process.

Chaotic scramble

I will start with a communication from Robin on December 31, 2019 as fires were spreading towards Mogo, 22 kilometres south of us, and threatening places further to the south and east. There was a strong probability that the winds would swing around and blow from the south fairly early in the day, which would put Robin's home—just 13.6 kilometres north of the oncoming inferno—and many others, right in the path of the fire. The conversation began at 7.39am with her simple, yet emotionally-charged statement, 'Not good over here, I'm scared.' She was home alone and suddenly facing the threat of a firewall. Seeing flames could be headed her way, she cried out for help. A friend came to her rescue and the two frantically set about blocking the downpipes and filling the gutters with water so Robin could evacuate when she needed, knowing she'd done all she could to save her home. Like so many others, she was surprised and alarmed by how early the fires had flared-up, and how quickly they were advancing upon our town. Though we were semi-prepared for an onslaught, it began before some had even risen from their beds.

Susan had her youngest son and his partner up from Melbourne for belated Christmas celebrations. They had arrived only to find the entire region blanketed in thick smoke. With a lazy sleep-in on their agenda for New Year's Eve morning, they were rudely woken at 6am and told they would have to leave as soon as possible and make their way toward their home in Melbourne, though the prevailing conditions and chaos on the roads made that almost impossible.

Another friend, Sylvia, had her ear glued to the radio keeping abreast of the latest on the fire, at the same time as she attempted to organise somewhere safe for her daughter and grandkids to escape to if the conditions worsened. She was thinking of heading to nearby Corrigans Beach, but only moments later, Susan, who had already evacuated to Hanging Rock Evacuation Centre, insisted that Sylvia 'get out now' and join her and the hundreds of others who were setting-up a makeshift camp there, surrounded by the odd assortment of possessions quickly grabbed from homes under threat.

By now, I had received word from my daughter Kelita—that they had been emergency-evacuated from the national park camping ground at Congo Beach, where she and the family had been staying since Boxing Day. They were quickly on the road, towing their old 80's caravan, desperately trying to get back to their home at Catalina, 43 kilometres north of where they'd been camped. After half an hour of driving, stopping and starting because of poor vision and road closures, they had only got as far as Tomakin before discovering that all roads heading north were blocked by fire and falling debris, with only emergency vehicles allowed through. Before they knew what was happening, flaming embers began raining down on them, setting alight spot fires too close for comfort, forcing all those gathered at the make-shift evacuation centre, to evacuate again. In a chaotic scramble, they made a beeline for the beach where they found a sea of vehicles crowded together in the usually quiet carpark, with people instinctively seeking refuge near the ocean.

I knew that 29 kilometres south of the rest of us, just seven kilometres from the Mogo fire, my eldest daughter Cassia and her crew had lost power very early in the morning as the fires devastated supply lines between Batemans Bay and Mogo. Phone reception was also very poor with only an occasional window of opportunity, when Cassia would head to high ground to keep an eye on the fire's progress. The last brief communication was a video sent from her mobile, showing thick plumes of dark, menacing smoke with orange flames leaping up toward the sky, fast approaching their home and property. For hours afterwards we heard nothing at all from them, and all we could do was hope and pray that they were safe and that their home had been spared.

Cassia told me afterwards that her, husband Garren and their two teenage girls Ella and Mia, had ensured they had a 'rough evacuation plan' in place.

Cassia

We had all of our irreplaceable items sorted and in a quick spot to grab. Our important paperwork had been condensed to one folder, and our campervan was semi-packed and ready to take off—or so we thought!

We'd had this plan for months, as we'd been threatened with the fire coming near us a number of times already. Like most people on the South Coast, we'd heeded RFS advice, but the threat of fire was such a constant that we, sort of, never really thought it would reach us.

But the day before New Year's Eve, I came home from work to burnt leaves falling everywhere around our house and yard. It was literally raining black leaves. This, paired with the scorching hot weather we'd been having, made me think seriously about the when and where of our evacuation plan.

None of us got much sleep that night, with the hot weather, big winds, smoke-filled air and checking the 'Fires Near Me' app all throughout the night. I was constantly getting alerts to all the suburbs that were being evacuated, and the warnings were getting closer and closer to us.

We woke early to get packing. At first, we were packing slowly in a 'just in case we need to evacuate' style. I had a look out at the top of the street where I could see the ridge in the direction the fire was coming from. I felt safe knowing we would have plenty of warning to get out.

By 9am the power was out and our internet was down. I was no longer able to keep abreast of what was happening. Our situation turned more drastic. It was up to us now, as to when we would leave, there was nobody else we could call or rely on. I tried to stay calm and think through what we had to do.

We really knew we were running out of time when the smoke became so thick that we were all forced to wear face washers over our mouths to breathe. With all of us attempting to remain calm, we quickly finished packing our car and camper. The sky had turned from a light orange glow to a dark, thick orange the next time we walked outside. It was like the fire was almost on top of us.

It all happened so quickly. I remember going to my lookout at the top of our street only 10 or 15 minutes after I'd last checked—and the ridge had completely disappeared in smoke.

The fire was coming.

During this time our packing had become more frantic. You start to look around your house thinking, 'What else do I need to keep?' But by then we had decided that we needed to get out of there fast, it had become too difficult to breathe, so there was no more packing.

Even though we'd had a plan, we never imagined that our time to carry it out would run out so quickly. It was as though one minute we were safe, and the next we were forced to flee. There was no time to wet down the house, no time to put the sprinklers on the roof. No more time! We *had* to leave.

We called our family to tell them we were evacuating and coming north to them, feeling relieved that we would all be together. But their reply was that they may be evacuating too because there were fires nearing them also. Garren and I are rational people, but it is difficult to think rationally when you find out that your fire plan has to change. We had to consider what roads might be closed and which way would be the safest route to get to safety.

With fire bearing down on us, we were forced to make a quick decision to head south, as we now knew there were fires to the west and north of us. We left with a quick prayer of protection over our home and the lives of anyone involved in this horrible situation. The road behind us was closed just 10 minutes after we made it through or we would have been trapped with nowhere to go.

Phew, that was way too close! Never in my life would I have imagined being in a car with my girls, following Garren in his car, fleeing an out-of-control fire that seemed to be chasing us.

Despite barely being able to breathe and not knowing where the rest of my family were, Garren and I felt a calm throughout the whole day. We were nervous for all our other family members who we couldn't contact; not knowing was definitely one of the hardest things, but we experienced a calm, nevertheless.

At the evacuation centre along the Moruya River, we were

surrounded by so many other evacuees—we couldn't believe how many people were being affected by these fires. I guess you don't comprehend the huge scale of the challenge until you find yourself in the middle of it.

The magnitude of the fires never really hit us until they were upon us, threatening our homes and lives. And until we saw just how many of our neighbours and strangers from other small towns were all seeking refuge. We'd had so many warnings and alerts, yet when the fire did come, it took us by surprise, and it came with such force that there was no containing it. As well, it hadn't been expected to hit until later in the day, so we all thought we had more time. It went wild so fast!

It was a sad sight, seeing how some people would be sleeping that night. Some had a mattress, others had nothing but a blanket on the hard ground. We had our campervan and were semi-organised. That felt good for our girls—one had packed light, the other, true to her teenage fashion nature, had wanted to take almost all her wardrobe with her—we compromised and had allowed her to take three suitcases.

As the long, hot day was dragging on and afternoon came, I soon realised I wasn't quite as organised as I had first thought. In the rush of things, we had forgotten to put the gas bottle onto the camper, so were unable to cook our food!

Little did we know at that stage, but our power was to be out for the next week and all the food in our fridge would be ruined as we went from one evacuation centre to another. For that one strange day, we had nothing at all to eat! All the supermarkets were closed, the town centre was a ghost-town—you couldn't be out in it, other than to get to the nearest evacuation point.

Later that evening a barbecue was hastily organised for everyone and we were each offered half a sausage on a slice of white bread. I tell you, even though we're normally really careful about what we eat—mostly gluten free and quality organic foods—it is amazing how good any food can taste when you're starving!

Camped beside the river, rumours were running wild the entire day. Because official news was so spasmodic or not coming through at all, we heard lots of stories. Some were about all the areas that the fire had taken out—including our entire estate! We wouldn't know, until it was safe to return home, whether we had a home to go to or not. And nobody knew when that would be.

Friends facing the fire

The same day that Cassia was evacuating, New Year's Eve, it was still quite early when my next 'Friends' report came from Robin, announcing that the fire front had passed by where she lives, and that she was feeling safe. The fire had come up the hill toward her on one side, and straight at her from the front. Firies had managed to save the homes in that area—though all the bush was gone. Unfortunately, the fire front passing Robin meant that someone else was now 'looking down the barrel of a gun' as the fire headed away from her and her Surf Beach neighbours. It didn't matter which way the fire turned, we knew someone, somewhere, was under threat and in serious danger.

At that time, I was still at Long Beach preparing to evacuate and wondering about the crazy timing of us moving into a place surrounded by trees and bush just days before pandemonium broke out. I stepped outside of our newly acquired Love Shack and began to film the sky looming over Batemans Bay and Batehaven. Replaying it now, I can clearly hear how scared I was with what I was seeing. 'It looks to be heading straight our way', I say, with thinly disguised panic in my voice.

I posted the video on our Friend's page and continued to do small tasks around the property to prepare for the fire. We had already done most of what was needed but with an overload of nervous energy to contend with, we had to keep moving. I also continued to look for things to pack so that if, or when, we evacuated, it wouldn't be too chaotic. I remained calm on the outside, forcing an atmosphere of peace within the Love Shack, making sure my Mum was doing okay and not panicking. She held up like a real trooper. She had her credit cards, driver's licence and a few valuables in a plastic clip lock bag in her shorts' pocket, in case we were forced to jump into the pool. As calm as we were making out to be, there was no denying the nervous energy in the room. We would have been forgiven thinking this was the end of the world.

A second video, taken only an hour later, is even more frightening, with flames and smoke forming a massive storm front that looked like a giant wave set to engulf the town. As I stood and took in the scene, a dread-filled thought crossed my mind. What if the evacuation centres, which we presumed were safe places, were actually in the fire path, what then?

Mum and I kept saying we would play cards or start a game, but it just never eventuated, we were continuously looking outside, watching the sky, checking for falling embers and making sure our things were packed. I guess we were both trying hard not to give in to fear and anxiety. By then, my daughter-in-luv (I don't do 'in-law') Lauren was really distressed, so her and our eldest son Ben with their baby River had come to our place. Jordan's children were also beginning to panic, so they decided to come to Granny and Pa's as well so we could all be together, with the adults supporting each other to make rational decisions while the cousins played together in what they considered a safe place.

'What are we still all doing here surrounded by trees and bushes that are ready to explode at the first sniff of fire?' I asked myself. But I knew the answer. There was no guaranteed safe place anywhere within cooee of the blazing monster. Even the short drive into the Bay could have soon been a concern, or even out of the question. With only one road into and out of Long Beach, we could be sitting ducks, yet the alternatives seemed equally frightening.

By 1:20pm we just seemed to sit there unknowing. We all longed to jump into our cars and begin a slow crawl into town. But it was too risky, it was too late to leave; we had no way of knowing what was 'out there'. Mum and I continued to fake calm for the sake of all the children, while Step busied himself around the property. To keep busy and occupied, while the little ones created games of their own, Mum and Jordan's eldest did some fancy sewing repairs to the felt rainbow unicorn I'd purchased at Vinnies just days before (don't ask).

It felt like night had fallen. The sky was still dark and foreboding, and with no power, there were no lights inside. Each time we ventured out to check the sky—our only guide as to what was happening with all communications shut down—hot, burnt, black leaves would fall from the sky and land around our bare feet.

The day was long and drawn out. Every hour seemed like a lifetime. Spasmodically my phone would beep to let me know, somehow, another message had gotten through. My phone wouldn't work for calls, yet Messenger was allowing a message through here and there. Susan messaged from the library to say she was safe, although sitting locked in the dark. I shot up a prayer for her.

Amazingly, the entire world had been alerted to Australia's plight, and many were watching the catastrophe unfold, but we were all without communication and had no awareness of the devastation experienced by our family and friends. Little did we know that by February 16, when all the fires were finally extinguished, two thirds of the entire Far South Coast would be burned, with our shire recording the most houses lost in the whole of our nation. We were totally unaware that fires would burn 79 per cent of the Eurobodalla, that four precious lives would be lost, that 501 homes would be destroyed and 274 homes damaged, with 1716 saved. No, at this stage, though things were getting really scary, we were yet to fathom the magnitude of what we were all facing.

'...the entire world had been alerted to Australia's plight, and many were watching the catastrophe unfold, but we were all without communication and had no awareness of the devastation experienced by our family and friends.'

As sporadic reports filtered in about the number of homes being destroyed by fire in Mogo, Malua Bay, Rosedale and Surf Beach, ash and smouldering leaves continued to fall on us at Long Beach. The next thing we knew, fires were erupting around Catalina, where my daughter Kelita lives. It was so surreal to be hearing fire reports on Mum's car radio and also by word of mouth, and then attempting to track them on the 'Fires Near Me' app. With reception dropping in and out, it was difficult to get a handle on what was happening in real time, and because many people were embellishing and exaggerating the facts, we couldn't be too sure about anything. It was like playing 'Chinese whispers', but on steroids!

At 2pm, Robin reported that she 'had a real close call as the southerly change came through. A neighbouring house up the road has gone, but my place is fine'. As fire crews gathered on her front deck to survey the situation and decide their next move, another message came through which simply said, 'Much too close for comfort!'

My friend Sylvia and her daughter (who has special needs) were still in her car. Her daughter was distraught and not coping well at all. They had been taking the lift up to the evacuation centre, only to have the power go out and be trapped there in the dark with strangers. A few kind men eventually managed to help her down the stairs and back into the car, where she sheltered with her Mum, picking up on the panic in the atmosphere and barely keeping it together. They were outside the evacuation centre without being able to head upstairs to discover if there was any real news. Not knowing what else to do, they decided to stay in the car and hope that a better plan would eventually reveal itself. They were very uncomfortable, but at least they felt safe with so many people round about. Little did they know that they would end up spending the entire night there, squashed uncomfortably among all the belongings they had packed into the vehicle.

I lost contact with the girls on Messenger again until after 6pm. It had been a weird afternoon, and to keep the littlies' minds off the fires, we all found ourselves playing in the pool to cool down, as if we were on a summer vacation.

At some stage on that crazy afternoon, miraculously a phone call got through. Unfortunately, it carried the devastating news that Kelita's house, and practically everything they own, was on fire and burning out of control. I was shell-shocked and stunned. When someone tells you that your daughter's house is burning down, it just doesn't compute. I posted another message on the Friends page, not knowing whether it had gone through or whether any of the girls would receive it: 'Kelita's house GONE!'

And then all communication and power were completely lost again. I remember standing at the window, waving my phone towards town, hoping to see one bar come up and allow me to make contact with my daughter, but it wasn't to be.

'We kept up a weird strain of chatter in the car, our nervous energy released with each heartbreaking observation of yet something else burnt, broken and destroyed.'

CHAPTER 4
No 'Happy New Year' here'

Without fanfare, without celebrations, without a thought to the date and bringing in the new year, we all remained on high alert until our adrenaline ran out and we went to bed totally exhausted. We knew this was how a lot of the South Coast households were 'celebrating' New Year—with many of them holed-up in cars and makeshift bedding at evacuation centres, while many more, like my Kelita, spent the night stunned and homeless.

It wasn't until the next morning, New Year's Day, that we had managed a fleeting connection with someone who let us know where Kelita and the family were staying. None of us had managed much sleep. Yesterday's heatwave had passed and the southerly had blown cool air in for us to go to bed—in the dark, without power or reception and without knowledge of where my children were and how many were safe. It was a very long night.

Early that first morning of 2020, there was to be no stopping us; Mum, Step and I jumped into Mum's little blue car and off we went. The trip into town was strange and other-worldly. The smoke and ash were much thicker and heavier than before, and the atmosphere was decidedly apocalyptic—like one of those end-of-the-world movies we watch but invariably regret doing so. No streetlights and no traffic lights were operating in the CBD. It felt like we had stepped back in time, 50 years or more.

Mum's car had air-conditioning. I'm not a lover of it normally, but the chill was so delicious we didn't want to get out, we just stared out at the hot, scorching day through the windows in the icy air in the car. Nevertheless, I was shivering, but I think it was from the shock of what we were seeing. The scale of annihilation that my eyes were attempting to take in, just did not make sense.

We kept up a weird strain of chatter in the car, our nervous energy released with each heartbreaking observation of yet something else burnt, broken and destroyed. We were making our way through what appeared to be a warzone surrounding us.

On our way, with eyes like saucers, we saw other places, here, there and everywhere, that had been wiped out. I couldn't help but notice how similar they all looked. Fire, it seems, is a great equaliser. No matter how posh or how poor the homes stood before, they all looked the same after the fire had demolished them to nothing but piles of brown rubble.

Searching for Kelita

Through the smoke and our own haze, we got to where we thought the family would be, but they weren't there. We soon found out that they had gone to visit the burnt remains of their home.

When we finally arrived there too, we realised that we had missed the family by minutes. We decided to take a look around before heading back to find them. As sad as it was, we wanted to see for ourselves, up close, what the fire had done. The scene was as pitiful as pitiful can be. All that was left of their modest, but comfortable, two storey brick home—which once bordered the bush at the end of a quiet cul de sac—was a smouldering pile of bricks and twisted metal. With bits and pieces of miscellaneous debris scattered about, the kids' swing set lying on its side was a stark reminder that a family once shared happy days here.

We felt sad and shaken by what we saw, and a little incredulous as well. We knew their home was in a precarious location should a fire ever threaten, but this? Before driving back to see our daughter, we drove around the immediate area and discovered at least another dozen homes that had been razed. One of our church friends lived over the hill from our daughter and we were fairly certain their place would have gone up because of where it was located. As we drove over to assess their situation, to our surprise and delight, their home was still standing amidst five or six blackened remains of what were their neighbour's homes. Unbelievable! Danni was standing in her driveway, her burnt out carport at her back, their side windows all shattered and their doorframe contorted. They'd saved their home, but only just. As we climbed out of the car to hug her, she told us it was her birthday.

We hurried down the road to see if our daughter had returned to where they were staying, and as we approached, we saw her oldest boy, Harper, out the front riding around on a borrowed BMX bike, with Kelita keeping a watchful eye on him. We couldn't jump out of the car quick enough, almost hugging the life out of them. We shed a few more tears and then we hugged some more—turns out this was to be a pattern for the next week; hugs, tears and more hugs. Eventually, we were led inside to catch-up with the rest of the crew, feeling relieved to be reunited again. A generator buzzed into action to enable us to a make a cuppa and sit down on the back deck together for a chat. About 20 minutes in, we had a very welcome interruption. Cassia, her hubby and their two daughters joined us after being out of contact for a couple of nail-biting days that felt more like a week.

We hugged and kissed and hugged some more, then over the next hour or two, we got down to sharing our experiences. These stories would be told and retold over the next month—and more. We were at the beginning of a time where we all breathed, talked and dreamed fire. It would be like nothing else existed besides fire.

'We were at the beginning of a time where we all breathed, talked and dreamed fire. It would be like nothing else existed besides fire.'

Cassia, her head shaking with the memory and shock of it all, told us that during their trip home from the evacuation centre in Moruya that morning, they had no idea what they would be coming back to.

Cassia

Driving through completely burnt out bushland all the way, it was the biggest relief seeing all the homes in our estate untouched! We couldn't believe it.

I went for a jog and was shocked to discover just how close it had come to our house. The fire had pushed to within a hundred metres of our property when the southerly, suddenly and mercifully, turned the fire back on itself, before driving it north, away from Mossy Point and surrounding suburbs like Tomakin and Broulee. Phew, what a relief!

It was miraculous. That southerly change came just in the nick of time for us!

With no power, phone or internet available, our family spent New Year's morning driving around to everyone's house that we knew—our friends, family and church family members, attempting to see who had escaped the flames and who hadn't. I don't think what we saw that day can ever sink in. It was just so weird to see where the fire had been, with some homes still standing, while others had been burnt down. The devastation was so widespread! For kilometre after kilometre after kilometre heading into town, all the bush was gone. Everything was black and brown, some of it still smouldering and pelting out smoke. It was impossible to fathom how much the fire had taken. We gave out a lot of hugs that day, accompanied by tears and had a sick-to-the-stomach feeling that persisted the whole day.

Calm to 'catastrophic'

After being reunited with family and then more painful sight-seeing and checking on other family members, this full-on, emotional New Year's Day was drawing to a close. With everyone else returning to their respective homes, Kelita and her crew stayed nearby with her husband's family. Three of our families headed north of the bridge to Long Beach, while Cassia and her crew headed back to Mossy Point, so grateful to have a home to return to after the touch-and-go situation of the day before.

The electricity network in the region had suffered extensive damage, leaving everyone without power—some for only a day or two, while others, especially those from the southern suburbs, for two weeks or more. We briefly heard a report by the CEO of one of the electricity supply companies, that it was estimated about 600 power poles on the South Coast alone would need to be replaced. He explained that each pole generally took a crew of four people anywhere from two to four hours to replace. While maths isn't my forte, it was obvious that line-crews had months of long days and nights ahead of them.

For the next two days, things seemed to settle down a bit for us. We didn't have property to survey nor did we need to estimate how much damage had occurred, like many on rural properties were doing. For us, there was little else to do but prepare for the next assault, which was predicted to hit in two days' time. The Bureau of Meteorology had issued warnings of even worse conditions for Saturday, January 4, so we had no time to rest or get complacent. The preferred term used by the Bureau was 'catastrophic weather conditions', and each time it was spoken you could feel the fear and anxiety in the atmosphere jump-up a notch or three. Even as I write this account, quite a number of weeks after the event, the word 'catastrophic' still sends a shiver down my spine.

We were busy preparing properties and organising to evacuate during those couple of days, living under thick smoke with a light ash still floating on the air, coating everything we owned, with whole black leaves covering the lawns, rooves and driveways. In between times we were either trying to get food, or trying to get fuel, neither of which were simple tasks. We had some supplies and not much petrol, and with all the shops and servos closed, it wasn't long before we started to run short. Fortunately for us, we were connected through Mace, to the famous Innes Boatshed takeaway business. Unfortunately for them, when the power outages occurred, they were forced to give away all of the home-caught fish and oysters from their commercial freezers to friends and family. While it was an extremely financially challenging time for them and for all the businesses in the area, we weren't the only ones to benefit from the Boatshed's generosity, with thousands of dollars-worth of seafood donated to the evacuation centres and to families who had lost homes. We were blessed to have been able to feast on fish and oysters for the next two days, about which Step is still raving.

Strange skies

The sky was doing strange things on Thursday afternoon and none of us could receive the official notifications of what we should do. Smoke was getting thicker and those tickle-in-the-throat sensations were constant. Ben's partner Lauren and I decided to head to the Long Beach Rural Fire Station, which was just a kilometre or so away, to see if we could be advised officially. We wanted to ask them what they were feeling about the situation and especially about Saturday's predicted catastrophic conditions. As we arrived at the fire shed, we saw cars parked haphazardly and people standing outside, milling about. We weren't the only ones who had that eerie suspicion that time was running out. Every face was turned towards the sky—looking and wondering. The uncertainty and unpredictability had everyone on edge.

This fire was a living thing—and an evil one at that—

waiting to strike when, and where, we least expected it. There was no playing with it. Our only hope was to get to somewhere safe. Allow me to add that 'safe' has become such a thought-provoking, emotional word. I used to be able to define it as somewhere where we were protected, not exposed to danger and risk or likely to be harmed. The word has taken on a whole new dimension during these volatile, unprecedented times, where we feel like we are running to, and then from, our 'safe' places.

With reports still filtering through about the devastation on the south side of town, and with only a relatively small, yet vulnerable, area to the north still untouched, a palpable sense of panic hung in the air. It was nerve-racking.

While at the fire shed, Lauren and I were confronted by an obviously shaken young man and his wife. Their story unfolded. He had been out fighting the fires, doing what he could to protect other people's properties, when his own home burnt to the ground. He looked at us helplessly with eyes that had taken on that glazed look that comes with shock and grief. He shook his head as if there were images in there that he couldn't escape from. No one could know what these heroic volunteer firies were going through 'out there' on that terrible battlefield. We stood together, stunned, saying nothing because there was nothing left to say. We hugged each other, mumbled our thanks, offered a hope-filled 'God bless', and we were on our way back home.

We travelled back the short distance without saying a word. We got out of the car with what must have been shock and fear written all over our faces as our family—Mace and Jordan and the five children, Mum, Ben, with his little son River in his arms, and Step—waited anxiously to hear what news we had brought back.

Jordan told me weeks later, that it seemed as though Lauren and I were gone for ages. 'We were willing you back. We needed to know you were safe, and we hoped that you would

> 'We stood together, a desperate huddle of people, struggling to stop our minds locking onto the worst-case scenario they were being inextricably drawn towards.'

bring back some miraculous report that we were all going to be alright.'

The waiting for our return was torturous for the families all gathered at the Love Shack, wondering what development of events, all outside of our control, had been predicted. Our faces relayed to them the precarious predicament we were in, long before our words confirmed it.

We stood together, a desperate huddle of people, struggling to stop our minds locking onto the worst-case scenario they were being inextricably drawn towards. These fires were burning with an unprecedented fury and nobody really knew what would be left when the smoke finally cleared. The reality of the situation hit us all like a freight train. We were under no illusion that the 'cavalry' would come riding in to rescue us just in the nick of time. There were too few people and nowhere near enough vehicles and equipment to cope with a disaster of this magnitude. We weren't levelling the blame at anyone, just trying to accept the reality of our circumstances and to sensibly steel ourselves for what was to come. Once again, we were trying to decide the best approach to evacuation, another unwelcome pattern of the summer.

To stay or leave

A constant message through these days, from our Mayor and the RFS, was to make a decision early as to whether to stay with your home or leave for an evacuation centre. And that either way, it was vital to be well-prepared and have a plan.

While we had stayed through the worst of the New Year's Eve conditions, the stories we heard from people who also stayed and were confronted by fire, were harrowing. They were all shocked by the intensity of the fire and many were saying that it almost cost them their lives.

Early next morning, on the Friday, before the worst of the conditions were predicted to hit, we imagined we had time to finish the last of our preparations and make sure our other two families were all set to go by that afternoon at the latest, but things heated up so quickly. Faced with rapidly deteriorating conditions, and with many accounts of ferocious and unpredictable fires playing on our minds, we collectively decided the best fire plan to undertake would be to leave. None of our families were in a good enough position to fight. The plan was to gather at the Coachhouse, near the Marina, which we were told was being used as one of the many evacuation centres.

Before this, Step had still been debating internally whether he should stay and protect the property, while I had been adamant that it was foolish to even consider the idea. We were later to discover this was a familiar dilemma for many families within our shire. It seemed the more I pushed for us to evacuate, the more he dug his heels in and said he was staying.

Communication was difficult. We were both angry. I guess that's what happens during grief. We were grieving for our daughter's loss and were still facing the possibility that more could just as quickly be taken from the rest of our family. It was exhausting. There was no reprieve, no time to sit and reason together. Nerves frayed, the future unclear, our safety unsure, I think we were bottling up our words, afraid that what we were fearing most, would come pouring out.

I eventually managed to get him to talk to me and tell me why he wanted to stay. He said that it was because the property was so well set-up with lots of water freely available, fire-fighting hoses, a back-up generator, and more. He felt terrible about leaving something with such a good chance of surviving the onslaught. I also think there is something within the male psyche that hates to admit defeat, something that wants to lash-out at whatever is threatening security and peace. This kind of behaviour had recently been displayed by a friend of ours. After his home burnt down, he saddled-up his ute with a tank, and went on a rampage into the fire, helping save many homes while screaming and yelling in anger at the flames. He had so much emotion bottled up that everything came pouring out in a heated rage.

Eventually the decision came down to this: after hearing so many gruelling stories since New Year's Eve and seeing the pleading on my face, Step decided that without any fire-fighting experience, and being on his own, staying would not be worth the risk. It was then that I breathed a big sigh of relief—I didn't want us to be apart during such unpredictable times. For me, staying together was the answer. Together, we could win any battle.

It may seem a tiny gesture, but we linked hands ever so briefly and just squeezed. It was us saying, without words, that we were on the same page. We were united again.

It is chaos in here!

Our situation was growing worse far sooner than anyone had foreseen. It was impossible to stay in the fire zone; Long Beach had been warned that we 'were next'. Not knowing what was going on, other than Susan's word last night to 'get out of there first thing in the morning,' we prepared to go.

Word was that Barlings was already on fire—and nobody had foreseen that! The fires that were predicted to flare on the Saturday, were already raging out of control early Friday morning. This did not instil any confidence in anyone after what our towns had all been through on New Year's Eve.

I cried again. Just quietly and calmly, but things were so out of control, with nowhere safe, and my family needed protection and nurturing. It was a big ask, a huge job and I wanted to be up for it. I wanted to be strong for them.

Whenever I had a moment to shed tears, I allowed them to come, releasing me to rise with renewed faith and resolve. I think I had God working overtime.

As we awaited the predicted onslaught, my 'Friends' messaging sparked up again. Sylvia let us know that town was still 'mad'. 'Stay out,' she urged, 'Fill and refill water bottles, have tin food or fruit, toilet paper, and essential personal items in the car. Be smart, don't drive around. It is chaos in here.' Oh, great timing—just when we were planning to head into it!

Robin makes a joke, reminding us of the healing power of laughter which brings relief for us all, 'I have plenty of toilet paper, I stocked up for the friends that didn't come.'

Long before now, tourists had been advised not to come. Once the New Year's Eve fire smashed through town like a violent giant on steroids, any tourists still here, were evacuated from motels and holiday accommodation. As a coastal town taken by surprise, we simply did not have enough personnel to care for the citizens of the Bay, let alone the massive influx of tourists that usually swell our town to bursting point.

Sylvia let us know that one of her neighbour's provided hot water so she could have a wash. With sweltering heat, ash covering everything (and I mean *everything!*), with black feet and no water, we were all starting to pong.

'I'm a happy girl now,' she let us know. We could relate. Nothing beats a refreshing shower! Sylvia, the dynamo, bursts into prayer, 'I pray against all the prophecies of man—we follow God's Word. We will stand with Jesus at our side. We will be wise; the fire may come but we are His. We are ready, but we won't be afraid. He is here. Just listen.'

Conditions continued to worsen, with the fire taking us all by surprise *again*. The two-days reprieve we thought we had, was suddenly swept away. The war was back on. There was to be no treaty. We desperately needed to get out while there was still time. There was a new sense of urgency about our packing. I dropped Mum to Lauren's to help babysit little River while

Lauren finished filling their cars.

Robin messages, 'I'm still in the dark. I have given all my food from the freezer away to the needy and to some who do have power.' Sylvia mentions that she has given away toiletries, clothes, linen, towels, food. 'Whatever I can find for people that have lost everything—it's only stuff.' Sylvia is good at snapping us out of our own funk and getting our eyes back on God and others. I'm grateful, once again, for this Friends page and the courage we help build in one another.

Eventually we were ready and the Long Beach families dribbled into town in our own little convoy. The women and children first, the men, doing the final checks on properties, following. Our cars were full and we felt we had done all we could. With more prayers, leaving things in God's hands, we headed to the evacuation centre to officially register our position.

Cassia and her family had also arranged to meet us at the evacuation centre but they would be coming up from the south. I prayed desperately that they would be able to make it this time—New Year's Eve's chaotic events that separated us, were far too painful and raw in my mind. They, like Step and I, would be using their own accommodation. They had their pop-up camper, still packed, and we had our much-travelled van, Buzz. However, we would all be registered together at the Coachhouse, where we would 'camp' outside the cabins assigned to the rest of our crew.

It was still pretty hectic with no power—apart from a few hours' reprieve here and there—no shops open, and only one servo open for business, and that only taking cash, no cards of any description. As you can imagine it was controlled chaos, with people lining-up for kilometres across the bridge. We made our way through the centre of Bateman's Bay, and down towards the south end of town. Sylvia had been right; it was a crazy bedlam of disorder. The roads were still blocked to the north past Long Beach, south towards Mogo and Moruya, and west towards Nelligen and Canberra. These were extreme times, times that will be almost impossible to forget. We were all perched vulnerably in the middle of it all, with no way out and nowhere to go.

'Looking at the bedlam, there was so much work ahead for almost everyone we spoke with—yet buoyed by others' generosity, there was also a sense of hope that our community would pull together in this and through this.'

CHAPTER 5
Time to lend a hand

Once officially registered as safe at the evacuation centre, we all 'set up house', unloading food into kitchens without power—loading ice into the fridges in an attempt to keep perishables lasting just a little longer—and making beds for little ones in the simple villas at the bayfront resort. Within the hour we were asked if we were available to help. The Coachhouse had been informed that Coles supermarket was open, but only for evacuation centre crews to come and get what they could, before it all ran out or the conditions worsened and it was impossible to get through. I am so proud of our boys, who jumped at the chance to help. They piled into cars and zoomed off, ready to load up and bring back whatever they could to feed the hoards. It must have been a very difficult task for the staff within the communal kitchen to work out what meals could be prepared, without power, for the hundreds of people forced out of their homes and into the once happy, holiday village.

When all our lads returned, Step said there were no cold goods: no fresh meat, no fresh milk, and from memory, no cheese, butter or eggs. There were lots of tinned foods, some bread, cartons of long-life milk, and other essentials like loo paper, sanitary pads, baby food and baby formulas. He said they were very grateful for anything they could get.

I remember awaiting their return, us girls leaning over the upstairs dining area rail, looking down at the full cars pulling up; men scrambling out to unload at the bottom the stairs. All food goods went into the kitchen, all other donations we set out in another room near the dining area. From then on, after dinner each night, evacuees and firies could take their next day's supplies of essentials—milk, tea, coffee, breakfast cereals, toilet paper, pads—and some not-so-essentials like mini bags of chips, Milo, and even some natural lollies for the kids.

With all of us gathered in one place at the Coachhouse, we were desperate for Kelita and her crew to join us. We knew they needed lots of TLC (tender loving care) and who better to give it to them than us, their kith and kin.

Lauren knew the Coachhouse manager, Kellie Whittington, and so calls were made to see what could be done to fit them in. With such severe conditions predicted, each passing hour saw more and more people arriving. Thankfully, Kellie did some tough talking to some 'powers that be' and was able to arrange a small unit for them. By now, Kelita and her family had already been shuffled to three different places in as many days since their house burnt down. They were thrilled to receive our messages urging them to come and join us.

Unfortunately, after all they had been through, they could barely muster the energy needed to relocate to the evacuation centre, so we were able to run them through the official drill of registering and securing four whole days where they wouldn't have to be moved on. What they needed, and were desperate for, was somewhere comfortable and easy where they could really relax and recover. They knew they would have a lot to think about and organise, as far as their future was concerned, and they certainly didn't need any extra stress in the picture. As it turned out, the Coachhouse really looked after them, taking them under their wing and continuously adding more days to their stay until they could find somewhere a little more permanent to move into.

Emergency housing fiasco

One thing that quickly became evident was that emergency accommodation became a fiasco. Some extremely generous and beautiful folk offered their homes for the homeless to rent at wonderful prices. Inappropriately, it also brought out the worst in others, and rental prices skyrocketed once it was announced that insurance companies would be footing the bill. Kelita, at one stage, was offered a home for $550 a week. She was devastated; they were still paying off their mortgage, had bills coming in, were up to their eyeballs in paperwork, red tape and everything else that goes with losing everything you own. Her hubby's work equipment had all been burnt, so he had no income coming in. The last thing they needed was for rent to eat up the little money their insurance company had given them to tide them over. It felt cruel.

Housing is a very real and common dilemma for many of the fire victims, but for now, suffice to say that Kelita's family were truly blessed to eventually find a private rental of a beautiful home at a very reasonable rate that should see their little family of five, settled for some months until they can get their head around where the heck they go from here. Thank God for emptyhouses.org and the genuinely kind souls who registered their homes. This kindness is of magnanimous proportion.

Meanwhile, back at the Coachhouse, things needed organising. The task of feeding us and all the other evacuees pouring in, took a team—it was 'all hands on deck'. And I truly thank God for this time. During the next week we were to help out in any way we could, with meals, clean-ups, fire-prepping and even setting up a further resource centre in the park.

Angel's wings

On Wednesday, January 8, provisions arrived on angel's wings. My beautiful cousin Matthew Kastelein had put the word out to his Central Coast community and within hours, had filled his trailer with donations for my girl and the other families in our church, who all lost their homes in the fires. A verse jumps to mind, 'He [God] makes the whole body fit together perfectly. As each part does its own special work, it helps the other parts grow, so that the whole body is healthy and growing and full of love,' (see Ephesians 4:16 NLT). We began to see this in action as everyone reached out—serving, helping, working together as one.

Matt sailed into the Coachhouse like a superhero with his truck and trailer bulging with donations from up north. We couldn't hug him enough. He had rallied these neighbours and friends and driven through fires and closed roads to get supplies down to us. It was acts of kindness like this, generous, selfless donations that took planning and effort and guts and stamina to perform, that really stand out for us now as we look back through the black. Matt may not know the full extent of what he did for us, but we carry this kindness in our hearts forever. Matt, and so many of our friends and family, near and far, came to our aid, meeting real needs and shining a light to guide us through a time that was very dark and bleak for those of us trapped within it.

Some we knew, others were strangers who remain anonymous—it may even have been YOU! Thank you, truly, from the depths of our being.

Looking at the bedlam, there was so much work ahead for almost everyone we spoke with—yet buoyed by others' generosity, there was also a sense of hope that our community would pull together in this and through this. Relationships were already being strengthened, people were beginning to reach out, resources were being shared——love was flowing.

I think of those lyrics penned by Bruce Woodley and Dobe Newton that we almost sing like an anthem, 'We are one, but we are many. I am, you are, we are Australian' and I see it in action everywhere. What a team we all make together. I want to grab everyone I see doing any small task that means so much and hug them and thank them. Together, we do make a difference. You matter!

Matt had gone the extra mile and had asked me for details of the families and put the word out about the kids' ages and clothes sizes and even brought a big box of gluten-free products for my daughter Kelita. Just looking at all these hand-picked, carefully-chosen items did our hearts so good. Matty goes down in fire history as a true legend who didn't stop at thinking about what could be done, but jumped up and did it!

I'm weeping... again, this kind of generosity, initiative and love helped so many get through this horrific time. I hope that Matt and his generous Central Coast friends, our new friends from afar, feel doubly blessed for what they did for us. And there was even a hand-written personal letter to me, filled with encouraging words of hope, from a lady who remains anonymous to me to this day.

It was a fun distraction setting up the new resource centre with Matt and my family. It gave us all something to occupy ourselves. We could be like caged lions at the evac centre— never knowing if it was safe to venture out, never knowing if or when or where the fires would strike again. Laying the goods out on tables it became quickly evident that Matt had covered everything! He had toys and games for the kids, bedding and towels, clothing and baby supplies, kitchenware, toilet paper and anything you could care to wish for. Enough for anyone within the centre to come and 'shop without money' as Harper called it.

Our little H was in his element. With a shopping bag spread open over one arm, he set to meandering around the centre gathering Spiderman, a toy truck, a big bag of chips, a T-shirt, some Lego. As he put each of these new treasures in his very own bag, he just marvelled that he could take it, and it was his, and he could keep it. His big blue eyes were sparkling.

Typing this now, I am also remembering the huge gift baskets Matt brought from a church up there—one for each of the four families in our church who had lost their homes. The baskets were filled with treats—Christmas treats like puddings and cakes and custard and cookies.

Healing through helping

Keeping busy at the Coachhouse helped to take our minds off the situation outside the centre—a very welcome reprieve. It gave us opportunity to serve, to meet others, to work as a team, to give back to Kellie, Gonz and the Coachhouse staff by way of thanks for all they were doing for us.

It was a bonding, healing, helping time and all our family will be forever grateful for the wonderful way in which we were looked after, so much so, more tears are flowing as I write this. I would love to be able to express what it meant to be able to be together, to be welcomed and to be useful—but I just don't have the words. The heart is full, but the expression of it nigh on impossible.

With plenty of mouths to feed and barely enough staff for the job, we were just some of many who jumped in and helped serve, and later, after dinner was over, to help with the cleaning and washing-up (no power equals no dishwasher). Water was heated on the gas stove in huge pots for us to bend over deep sinks and wash dishes that were piled up above our shoulders. And all by candlelight. From then on, we were unofficially 'on-call' whenever help was needed, and were pleased that we could be there to support the management and staff who always went above and beyond for everyone there.

A counsellor friend of mine phoned to offer her condolences about our family's loss, but at the same time she also offered some wise advice about helping the children recover from trauma. She pointed-out that the main influence in a child's life is invariably the 'big people' in their world.

'How a child's parents deal with their own grief is often an accurate measure of how a child will manage theirs. If they observe the adults around them crumble and fall to pieces, then they might presume that to be the appropriate response to the situation. But while the big people are able to display courage, optimism and resilience, the children are more likely to adopt a similar response and mimic what they see.'

I found this to shine often within their unstructured play—when they would be playing 'mummies and daddies', mimicking what they'd seen and heard from us. Don't get me wrong, never once did we trivialise anyone's grief, or the methods they employed to express it, nor did we add extra burdens or demands on our adult children, also struggling to process their loss. Everyone was free to express themselves, yet we all remained conscious of how much we may have been influencing our children and their ability to cope with adversity. Sometimes it was as simple as stalling a conversation until little ears weren't present.

I learned years ago, that fixing my eyes on helping others was one of the greatest ways to help 'fix' myself, for want of a better term. Little did I know that by volunteering to help at the Coachhouse, I would 'catch' that servant-heart again and spend the following weeks finding ways to serve my wider family, those friends from our church, Southland, who had lost their homes and almost every possession they owned. God grabbed a hold of my heart there in that Coachhouse.

To be honest, before arriving at the Coachhouse I'd been feeling helpless about my own situation and that of my children, being kind of 'holed-up' at Long Beach watching and waiting. Staying at the Coachhouse provided the space I needed to begin reaching out to help others, and that journey, thank God, is a continuing one. Later, after we left, I spent weeks gathering food, clothing and essentials, finding funding resources and using Buzz as a delivery van. Once everyone I knew had as much as I could assist with, I went on to do what I do best— sitting one-on-one in coffee shops and listening—allowing stories to be told and validated. I continue to enjoy this type of 'ministry'. It comes most naturally to me. And it is helping people get out of their houses and process their experiences, while bringing reassurance that someone will listen, all while supporting the small, struggling businesses in our towns. A win, win—my favourite.

Of course, it is seven weeks on as I collate this and there are now many organisations doing so much more for the people of our community on a grander scale. A huge hats-off to our Council. Our Mayor and her team worked around the clock during this frantic time. With their own homes to defend, they put in long hours to ensure things were replaced or up and running as soon as was humanly possible under these extreme conditions. I don't think any of us could thank our firies, our volunteers, our rescue workers, our incredible team of workers who served tirelessly on behalf of this community. I'm overwhelmed with what they did for us. When you look at the cold, hard statistics of what went on here, it is nothing short of a miracle that so much was saved, especially human lives, that we will be forever grateful.

Knights in shining armour

I don't know how it happened so quickly, but services were set up as fast as they could muster—Red Cross, St Vinnies, Anglicare, Rotary, Country Women's Association to name a few.

There are teams of helpers who have arrived from elsewhere like knights in shining armour—in ships, tanks, planes, choppers, trucks and utes. One such is BlazeAid, a volunteer-based organisation that works with families after natural disasters. Working alongside the families, the volunteers help rebuild fences and other structures that have been damaged or destroyed, also helping to lift the spirits of people. I like their motto, 'Not just rebuilding fences, but helping rebuild lives'. My mate Max is raving about them at the moment. Max saved his Termeil house, even though it was hit by the fires twice, just four days apart. One fire roared up and took out two sides and the back of his property including sheds, stables, pens and cottages, with Max fighting against the mighty beast relentlessly to save his home. A volunteer firefighter himself, just a few days later while Max was out saving other houses, unbelievably, the fire returned to his property, hammering it again, this time from the front, until everything he owned was burnt to the ground right up to the front steps of his home. How his house survived, is a combination of mighty firefighting effort and sheer miracle! Now BlazeAid are helping rebuild the fences all round.

Another is Samaritan's Purse, a Christian not-for-profit disaster relief organisation. With volunteers from all over the world—I've met some from France, USA and Canada—these amazing, generous people are getting stuck in and helping clear blocks. With hearts of gold and the peace of God, they simply serve in any capacity they can, and all as a free service.

Last week they were at my friend Amanda's block to help cut down the dead trees so clearing could begin after her house, car and everything she owned were burnt down. 'They saw the devastation on their news at home in their own countries and wanted to come all the way here to help!' Amanda enthused. 'Beautiful, beautiful people!'

Seven weeks on, our friend James, who stayed to defend his property and almost lost his house, has been struggling with every kind of emotion you can think of. Unable to live in his home due to the huge hole in the roof and the burnt-out beams, he has been bunked down at his girlfriend's house.

James

At first, I couldn't spend more than an hour back on my property. It was too depressing and too daunting. I think I'm struggling with post-traumatic stress disorder (PTSD), unable to recover after witnessing such a terrifying event, and I've been unable to sleep. When I close my eyes, I keep seeing the flames heading toward me.

It's like my home has let me down. This was meant to be my safe haven from the world and now it is almost all gone and totally unlivable. Until this week, I hadn't been able to settle into my paid work or begin the clean-up at home. I was in limbo and didn't know how to deal with the emotions I was struggling with.

Assessors have since been in and the entire roof and the beam structures need removing and replacing. It is going to be a big job, removing the roof and having to replace the whole lot.

Once the assessment was done and I had an idea of what I was faced with, I kind of went into hyper mode. I've been doing 12-hour days at the block, trying to get my gardens in order and work out how I can begin again. It was all too daunting and overwhelming until I heard that there was assistance available. What a relief to find people who want to come out and help me. I've got a team coming to help me on Monday. Samaritans Purse is coming to my rescue.

I, Chrissy, watched this busy team scurrying over another block, like ants. Organised, working as a team, serving for the greater good. Another friend posted about them on social media, 'Samaritan's Purse is the most amazing organisation I have ever dealt with. Out of all this heartache and sadness and endless days of anxiety not knowing where to start to get this place back to where it used to be, today came growth and renewed hope. Free of charge, they worked for hours to get our property back to some sort of organisation along with a shoulder to cry on, which has given me renewed strength to keep moving forward.'

Witnessing genuine acts of random kindness speak volumes to the children. More on my kids later, but again it is enough to say that what children see, they often emulate. Within all the confusion and uncertainty, and their own pain and stresses, my (adult) children rose to serve others right where they were at during our evacuation. Not for glory or accolades, they merely served with a sparkle in their tired eyes and cheer in their encouragement. And all the while, their children watched. What will the children remember amidst these fires? What lessons will they take with them through life? Hopefully, that kindness and service toward others is not only a good thing, but the right thing.

The anxiety of children

Back to Friday, January 3—and we were facing the next round of challenges. It was time to put the children to bed but watching fires flare up was no way to settle them. There at the Coachhouse, after a full-on day, everyone's nerves were frayed. Yet we concentrated on doing all we could to 'go through the motions' in an attempt to keep everything as normal as possible for the sake of the children. But they were not fooled. They are clever little Vegemites and were picking up on the vibes. When the sky turns orange through the smoke and the distant hills light up with flames, there was no denying the situation we were in.

It was stressful seeing some of the children showing signs of trauma in different ways—being clingy toward their mothers, outbursts of anger, bedwetting that hadn't occurred in years, nightmares, and putting their hands over their ears when they couldn't cope with what they were hearing. Also, the children had heard that there were looters on the grounds and the thought of this had scared them further. Some didn't want to go to bed until they knew all the doors were locked and their parents (and toys) were inside. It is a sad state of affairs when people come to prey on the broken. A couple of young guys had been caught loitering around the place. Rumour got back to us that they were found with stolen goods before even getting out of town. This was good news for the children; in their minds it meant all the looters had been caught. They needed some peace of mind—they deserved at least that much.

Harper and London had already lost their home and everything in it, to see another fire-front on the mountains flare up right on bedtime was so frightening. The adults were struggling to process our situation at the time—what hope did their young minds have of fathoming it all. Sylvia got a message through, 'We stand in the gap for our children, our town, our family, our friends and for the lost and seemingly forgotten. May peace and grace rain down around our little ones tonight.'

My friend Jenny Phillips, whose own grandchildren had been evacuated to Ulladulla, also sent a message to remind me to 'encourage the kids to draw. As they draw, kids chat and tell the story about their pictures. In this way they express their emotions and this will help in a small way with the upheaval they are experiencing.'

My beautiful counsellor friend Donna, staying updated through my online posts from her home in Victoria, sent me through a message.

Donna Hunter

It is important for the kids to hear adults talk about positives—don't let the kids hear too much talk about the negatives; continue to give them lots of reassurance. This doesn't mean lying, it means focusing on hopefulness and giving them space for whichever way they want to communicate how they are feeling. Listen with your ears, heart and hands and don't shut them down.

Ensure them that the adults are going to protect them—even getting them to draw pictures with hopeful messages and thank-yous to give out can be empowering for them. Trauma is experienced when a person feels helpless in a situation like this, so getting them involved in helping in any way will have a positive effect long term.

It was great advice to heed during the days in the Coachhouse. Interestingly, the second week after we were able to return to our homes, Cassia's youngest daughter Mia asked if she could come and stay and help me gather things for others. She was a dynamo. Mia has always had a soft, servant heart, a gift for giving and an intuitive sense of when others are hurting. For all her 12 years, she is an amazing human. It was a real hoot having her with me, she lifted my spirits as I watched her take such great delight in 'shopping without money' for her extended family and friends who had lost everything.

You have to remember that we were without power and supermarkets and income for a time, so being able to gather essentials was a necessity, especially to those who had nothing left but what they could gather at the evac centres. Organic baby food and natural wipes, charcoal toothpaste and bamboo toothbrushes, hairclips, tinned foods, nappies, organic food bars—all of these were found by Mia. She would dig through the boxes and come up with the good stuff. And of course, tinned tuna. There were stacks of it leaning precariously upon the tables, in the boxes and scattered throughout some of the other foodstuff. There was never a shortage of tuna.

Mia and I did this for two days, and then she would sit on my mats at the Love Shack and divide it all into bags for those she had in mind. And then the two of us would go out in Buzz and deliver it all like it was Christmas. And we would hug people; Mia gives wonderful hugs. Yeah, I believe my kids are raising their kids to be beautiful, generous and kind-hearted— and this thrills this Granny's heart.

Speaking of tuna, I have to tell you about my friend Julie. We became mates after Julie won one of my books at a Christmas party a few years back, as life-events would have it. Since then, we have been spontaneously meeting for cuppas together in local cafes, as she's one of those gals who can jump to an invitation so quickly that we're holding cuppas in our hands within half an hour of the call. I love that kinda gal!

During the fire threats throughout November and early December, we would share stories, ideas, vision and all that great stuff we bounce off, encourage and champion one another with. We would also discuss 'distant' fires, but December 31 changed that.

'As we were leaving, we saw flames leaping up into the air as trees ignited. Those black leaves that had been falling for days were swirling all around us and we had to dodge branches on fire.'

Julie Steedman

Like everyone on New Year's Eve morning we fled our house and headed to the beach. I guess just the fact that my sentence can begin with 'like everyone, we fled our house,' reflects the magnitude of our strange existence where fleeing in fear was the 'norm'. But we were luckier than some. We had a box of special things already packed as we had just returned from three weeks' holiday the night before.

On the day of the fires heading straight for us, we packed this box, our safe, our laptops and two bags of clothes that were in our entry from the night before as we left them to climb up the stairs to bed.

I woke our 16-year-old, she grabbed her mouse and I grabbed the dog. I went upstairs to empty my husband, Mat's backpack on the bed—and pulled photo's off the walls as I left. We bundled into the car and waited for Mat.

Mat, after running around pulling items away from our house that may catch fire, hooked up his boat as he was worried it might allow the fire to spread to next door and hinder access for firefighters. I was thinking, 'the insurance is worth more than we would ever get if we sold it!' And we fled towards Pretty Beach.

Our story, like a lot of stories you read on paper, can give the impression of sounding a calm and orderly affair, but everything was far from calm or orderly that morning. As we were leaving, we saw flames leaping up into the air as trees ignited. Those black leaves that had been falling for days were swirling all around us and we had to dodge branches on fire that were hurtling from the sky.

I'm not sure what most of us expected when we arrived at various evacuation points towards the ocean, but the warzone seemed to follow everyone. When we hear the term 'fleeing' we imagine it is always to a 'safer space'—on New Year's Eve, there didn't seem to be any safe spaces anywhere.

Within an hour of arriving at Pretty Beach, the heat was so intense that we were forced to head closer to the water. As we cautiously rounded the bend, we saw an ember hit a tree on Pretty Point and watched, stunned, as it burst into angry flames. Things were too dangerous here to go any further forward. Fire was everywhere. We quickly grabbed our phones to call for help—only to find they were useless with no internet, no phone reception and no SOS. My smart phone now became a camera to record events as they unfolded.

Within minutes the whole Point was ablaze and we all prayed it didn't spread to our little group and force us into the freezing water. There was so much going on—the heat, the darkness, the smoke… everyone here experienced that. The fear, the anxiety, the worry… everyone here experienced that, too.

Those of us who have endured, and somehow miraculously survived, these intense months on the South Coast, know exactly what I'm saying. Everybody was in a panic by the time we were gathered at evacuation points. Watching things burst into flame around you isn't something you can be calm about. And we were in such intense heat! We knew the fear, the anxiety, the worry firsthand and we didn't know what to do with it. Surviving this crazy time almost seemed impossible during the heat in the middle of the fire zone.

That first hour turned into six long hours before the worst was over and we had any suggestion that the threat had eased. Attempting to think clearly and make wise decisions while our hearts were racing and our heads reeling and the earth boiling was no easy feat. We eventually decided to return to our home, we figured the worst of everything was over and we were safe to head to the safety of our beautiful home.

It was wild out on the roads. Never had we seen anything like it; we couldn't believe that the main road into our street was on fire. We started to drive toward home only to find George Bass Drive was alight. It devastated us that we couldn't go home. We couldn't go any further forward as the fire forced us back to where we started.

This proved to be a blessing in disguise, as when we tried to head home again about 30 minutes later, dodging and weaving our way through what seemed like a battlefront, we found our house was a pile of smouldering besser block walls and twisted metal roofing.

Had we arrived that half-hour earlier, we would have witnessed our house burning down.

Our house couldn't be saved, but Mat's workshop was still burning when we arrived. It was near to the fence and could easily cause the fire to spread, so he rushed to our neighbour's house to try to stop it. Mat was intent on saving this house—he went into overdrive and just wouldn't stop. There were all sorts of combustible materials in the shed, but Mat was manic. He was determined to stop the fire spreading—which gratefully was successful.

Our home was the last to burn on our street.

Five houses were lost, five families' lives just got turned upside down. The stress continued for all those without homes. With no power, with no communication getting in or coming out, no stores open, no fuel, we 'shopped' in friends' pantries so we could eat.

But don't feel sorry for me! We are luckier than some. We have insurance; we have enough insurance to start again. We will be looked after.

Yet both my husband and I are self-employed. Neither of us were quite ready to go back to work for some time; we were surrounded by trauma and we had to work out our way forward. We had no income, but the bills keep coming! I had to swallow my thoughts of 'I don't need help' and allow friends and strangers to donate money, food and toiletries. Instead of me lending a helping hand, I was holding out my hand. It is a very strange feeling to be on the receiving end. It is difficult to hold your hand out and take what others are giving to you out of the goodness of their hearts.

But again, don't feel sorry for me! We celebrate our 'little wins' when we find items we thought were gone but are found. Like my jacket. I thought it had gone up in smoke but we discovered it under the dog blanket in the back of the car one day. I could have done a happy-dance over a jacket.

I know Chrissy calls them 'kisses from heaven'—these tiny victories where it feels like God is reminding us of His love for us, blessing us in simple ways that mean so much to ourselves, but may not be noticed by others. We celebrate all the 'heart' people out there bringing in donations and distributing them. We celebrate that we get to buy new things and create new memories and recreate the history that goes along with that item.

Why mourn when we can celebrate? I'm not downplaying what we've been through. Our loss was huge! Devastating! And in a weird way, cleansing! Our trauma was real, the whole community is traumatised! But our spirit is rippling under the surface and we will rise above this. We are bent but not broken and my little family is closer than it ever was before. So don't feel sorry for me!

I am determined that I have the power to rise from this. Through this journey I am determined to gain more than I lost. Don't get me wrong, this is tragic, but it will not define me! I always think positively, well almost, and I try to see the lesson in everything that happens in my life. I'm struggling with the why for this one, but I'm sure it will all make sense one day when I look back to see how much my life has changed from this moment... this event and the days that followed.

What I've learned is to be ready when fires or similar are

nearby, it is easier to pack items of importance with a clear head. Pack as if you are never coming back. I didn't know that then and we left things behind, as I truly thought we were coming back to our house.

No house is worth your life. I loved my house, but I do not regret leaving it. I've learned that what doesn't kill you makes you stronger and that on any given day you can step out the front door of your home and your whole life can change. How we react to that change is our choice. My family and I have chosen to see the good and to move forward, carrying any lessons that we can with us.

We won't rebuild on our land. Our house has been demolished and our block will be cleared, but we don't want to go back there. We want to start again. As Mat and I and our daughter sat together discussing what our options were, my daughter said, 'Why don't we downsize'. We had a big house and my son has already moved out. Mat and I had a 10-year plan to downsize after our daughter finishes school and moves out. When she suggested we bring that plan forward, it seemed like the most natural thing in the world to do.

So we set out to find a house. I already had an idea of what I wanted and what we needed. Our needs had changed since we bought our beautiful home all those years ago. We didn't need as much space. And we were blessed to find the perfect house, overlooking the ocean so one day I could watch wales—one of the goals I had for our next home. We were able to purchase the home with our insurance money and the owners allowed us to move right in. So we are renting the home from the owners until the sale goes through, and setting it up just the way we like it, with some of our old treasures and lots of new ones. We are luckier than some. We had enough insurance to start again—and we all love our new home.

During the first month or so, we received so much support from our family, our friends and this wonderful community. We received boxes of donated clothes, shoes, toiletries and pantry items, we received enough baked beans, spaghetti and soup to last a lifetime. We also have enough tuna to last two lifetimes! Ha-ha.

The Resource Centre was well-stocked with tuna. Tinned tuna of every description—in brine, in spring water or organic oil—with peppercorns, chilli, garlic or lemon, with sundried tomatoes or spring onions and the list goes on. So please, please, please, if there's ever another time of need, PLEASE remember… we have enough tuna!

Full circle of fire

Serendipitously, for me, it was during this month of buzzing around helping those affected by the fires that I was reminded by a few families of how my initial Buzz-journey began. It was back on February 9, 2009, more than a decade ago, just two days after another of the worst bushfire disasters in Australian history, the Black Saturday Fires in Victoria. On that day, Step and I, after we had sold or given away almost all that we owned, set out to travel Australia in our van called Buzz. Yes, this is where our journey began; led straight into smouldering bush fire zones to volunteer in a relief centre in Healesville Victoria 11 years earlier.

After months there, serving alongside the locals in the main relief centre, distributing food, clothing, essentials and tinned tuna (sound familiar?) we also learned a lot about the power of a hug. Just as we are now, we were reminded back then of the powerful ministry of empathy and genuine love. My first book *Falling Up Stairs* tells more of our experiences in the aftermath of Black Saturday.

'You who sit down in God's presence, who spend the night in his shadow, say this: "God, you're my refuge. I trust in you and I'm safe!" That's right, he rescues you and shields you from deadly hazards. His huge outstretched arms protect you—under them you're perfectly safe; his arms fend off all harm.'

(Psalm 91:1-4 MSG)

CHAPTER 6
Fire fronts are everywhere

Let's return to the timeline of events during the peak of the South Coast fires. The dreaded Saturday, January 4, 2020 finally arrived and with it a very subdued, yet ominous feel about the day. After yet another night of fires raging relentlessly, I was up before dawn—though who would know the time—as the sky remained dark with clouds that we hoped were thunderclouds filled with water, but were big, heavy, black, huge plumes of smoke.

Little did I know then that rain wouldn't come for yet another month! I think if any of us knew we had to endure another month of drought, fire threats, intense heat and another fire front sweeping up through Moruya, we would have collapsed under the weight of it.

Things were still so raw. We could barely process what was happening. Every now and then someone sheltered at the evac centre would snap and lose the plot, yelling and swearing and running around like a chook with its head cut off. You sort of expected it really. Months of tension had been trapped inside. Just like the atmosphere around us, some had tempers that flared up and exploded like a bonfire.

That morning, because sleep was almost impossible during a lot of those nights, Step and I decided to head over to Hanging Rock Evacuation Centre while our crew were all asleep in their cabins. There were people everywhere. Misplaced, homeless, evacuated, stunned people—everywhere. Not just hundreds, but a thousand or more of them.

'Fire is an equaliser—we had all been reduced to the few belongings that fit into our vehicles and were united in our common uncertainty of our futures and the relief that we were all still alive.'

A small corral had been made against a fence, with horses neighing without understanding. Dogs on leads, cats in cars getting snuggles; children finding pockets of grass to play on— able to make a game of any situation. It was surreal to witness. It all resembled the world's worst holiday park. Yet, everyone was smiling—the human spirit is so resilient. I couldn't believe that most people were attempting to make the most of a bad situation and were determined not to dwell on the chaos surrounding us all. We were all in the same boat, more or less. Fire is an equaliser—we had all been reduced to the few belongings that fit into our vehicles and were united in our common uncertainty of our futures and the relief that we were all still alive.

We met a man who had lost his home; angry that his wife had left him alone to defend it. There was some serious grief-blame going on and we just nodded and eventually hugged him when he was all talked out. Step was able to calm another man in a panic. It was 8am I think, I'd been awake since 4.40am, when seven spots of rain had fallen on the roof of Buzz and I was excited to think it might keep going and turn into something real. I went upstairs: awaited the early announcement as to what our predicament was and what was to come. We all knew that the fires were gaining power. These firewalls were huge. They were expanding, twisting, turning and they were taking so much ground that they were joining. They were ferocious and there was no playing with fire. There remained no good news. 'Fire-fronts are everywhere. All roads are closed. Amidst the instability and uncertainty, everyone is dealing with things as best they can.' Basically, we were informed of what we already knew—that we were still without power, petrol and supermarkets and that we remained hemmed-in by fire.

It is difficult to describe the feeling of wondering if you are going to survive, or wondering if you will have a home to return to, or wondering where the fires would strike next, or wondering what the day in front of you would bring, let alone the day after that. It seemed an impossibly ridiculous situation, yet there we all were, gathered together like rejected carnival workers after the fair had moved on.

It was an eye-opener for me to realise how many were sleeping outdoors on the grass or propped up in their cars, amidst their possessions—pillows and paperwork and pets.

Famous Aussie generosity

What eventually reduced me to tears was the generosity us Aussies are famous for. This one particular incident will stay in my mind forever more.

As I was collecting a box of toys for my three grandkids who'd lost everything in the fires, the volunteers were going out of their way for me. Their kindness was beyond what was expected of them. So much time was taken by three particular volunteers who'd been assigned to give out toys from inside a shipping container. My little London, Kelita's three-year-old daughter, adores the movie *Frozen* and anything associated with it. Her favourite colour is blue, like Elsa, she can sing *Let it Go* without prompting and has travelled to Canberra to watch the entire story performed on ice—all the while perched on the edge of her seat with a crooked crown upon her head and her nylon blue gown overtop of her warm clothes. When I saw a *Frozen* toy in one of the boxes, I told the team my granddaughter would love it. I gathered that toy, a plastic lizard and blocks for the baby and then some creative toys for my big boy, things he had to work out and put together so he could stay busy and use his overactive mind for something constructive and positive—like a model plane and some Lego.

Once my box was full, I struggled to carry it across the grass toward the entrance to the Coachhouse—I had originally only popped in there to be able to surprise my grandkids with one or two toys, yet the volunteers wouldn't hear of it, they just kept loading me up until my box was overflowing. But here is the real winner—one of the women who had been helping find age-appropriate toys from the shipping container, chased me, yes, literally chased me, along the sports fields where everyone was camped, calling after me. She had found another *Frozen* toy, a boardgame, after I'd left and she really wanted London to have it. That did me in. I tell you, I just bawled. Acts of kindness like that, right there and then; they mean the world. Who does that for a stranger? I was so overwhelmed. She kept asking me if I was okay. I was more than okay, but how does one express such gratitude? We hugged long and hard.

Not much further past that hugging point, I needed help to get the box back to our accommodation—it really was bulging with gifts and awkward to carry, so I'd phoned my son Ben to drive down and get me. Though it was only a short way away, I think I was too overcome, I'd had so many emotions raging through my body those past weeks, it was impossible to contain them all at times. It had felt great dumping that box of goodies on the back seat of his car and being able to ride the rest of the way. The grandkids rushed out to meet us when we arrived and couldn't believe the treasures, celebrating with great shouts of joy. Among the toys, the baby Lennox loved a simple slap band and H went crazy over a footy. Watching my grandkids' faces as they went through the box, was sheer gold. And I was again overcome by the gratitude expressed for everything they received.

God will save the day

It was D-Day, the day predicted to wipe out Long Beach where we lived. Robin had been praying and sent through on our Friends page, 'My word for us girls today is this, *God will save the day*. Pray it, proclaim it, believe it.' Sylvia added some practical advice, 'Yes, God will save the day, but He also tells us to be wise and not to be complacent or foolish.' I felt good that we were all out of Long Beach. We were in one of the safest places we could be—albeit in the centre of a town with fires raging in all directions around us.

I shared on the Friends page about the night we'd had volunteering. It had lifted my spirits. Robin responded with life-giving encouragement, 'God bless you Chrissy and Step. Keep on with the good work of being Jesus' hands and feet in there. Go girl, go in His strength. This is a day of victory not disaster. Proclaim it out loud.' Susan responds, 'My Father will keep us safe under his wings.'

Robin had been to our church to pray. 'Last night I saw a vision of a huge eagle hovering over the Bay protecting us. God will shelter us under His wings and we can take refuge in the shadow of the Almighty. Psalm 91.'

As world news continuously reported on the day's predicted disaster, my phone beeped with messages from friends from all over the globe. One message bringing encouragement was from our beautiful, young friend Esther, who used to live on the South Coast and had recently been visiting with us. 'Keep on keeping on guys. May God fuel your strength and make you shine as messengers of peace, love and hope, both as you give and receive.' I felt that you couldn't really sum up the situation better than that. Interestingly, she also sent us Psalm 91:

> You who sit down in God's presence, who spend the night in his shadow, say this: 'God, you're my refuge. I trust in you and I'm safe!' That's right, he rescues you and shields you

from deadly hazards. His huge outstretched arms protect you—under them you're perfectly safe; his arms fend off all harm. (Psalm 91:1-4 MSG)

This Psalm wasn't new to us during this time. It first grabbed my attention during our last Soul Sisters' weekly get-together for 2019 in November. Not surprisingly, it has come up continuously throughout this strange fire season; popping up regularly on our Friends page. And when we were to walk into church for the first service for 2020 the next day— in the dark during a blackout— it would be referred to again by my son-in-luv Garren, who is the leader of Southland Church.

It was bringing us a lot of comfort during some of the scarier times. Robin discovered that The Passion version suited us best. Here's the final three verses of Psalm 91:

For here is what the Lord has spoken to me: 'Because you have delighted in me as my great lover, I will greatly protect you. I will set you in a high place, safe and secure before my face. I will answer your cry for help every time you pray, and you will find and feel my presence even in your time of pressure and trouble. I will be your glorious hero and give you a feast. You will be satisfied with a full life and with all that I do for you. For you will enjoy the fulness of my salvation.' (TPT)

It was interesting that when emergency kits were being discussed during the height of evacuation planning, one of us thought it a good idea to add the Bible. Deciding what should go in and what shouldn't, was a bit of a challenge so common-sense prevailed and we agreed to have on hand a prepared box filled with some essentials like batteries and torches, water and some tinned food, packs of nuts and dried fruit and long-life milk. Added to this, a first aid kit stocked and ready, tissues and basic toiletries and scissors. Of course, Rescue Remedy and

Arnica, natural first aid for any shock or trauma, were among our essentials. Much later, I ended up gathering some face masks from the army while they were manning the Resource Centre, but by then, two weeks after the worst of the fires, the smoke seemed to be clearing.

From the fireground—January 4, 2020

We are alert and desperate to know what is going to happen. Step and I keep pushing our 'let's be positive and believe for the best outcome for today' barrow, while many others within the Coachhouse struggle to see any sign of a silver lining, anywhere at all. Nine o'clock ticks over, then 10, and then 11, without any dramas in our region to speak of. Surely, we can get through one lousy day without any more destruction! The temperature is high but nowhere near what had been predicted. Also, the wind, which is always a major concern, is blowing from the east and not the west. I'm so thankful for this one small, yet significant mercy!

From our vantage point, we can see clearly to the north and watch if any fires erupt and threaten us from that direction. The best-case scenario is for the wind to keep blowing—as it is predominantly from the east—and for fire crews to have the opportunity to contain and mop-up fires around places like Catalina where the most recent damage occurred. The evacuation centres are close enough to be a concern, but only if the wind blows-up and stirs these fires into life. For now, with fires turning in upon themselves, helicopters and planes fill the air, scooping and carting water all morning. The sound of sirens is constantly in our ears and evacuation plans, in case of spot fires, are continuously discussed. We are beside the sea; as 'safe' as we are going to get.

Now it's mid-afternoon and the wind is starting to intensify, causing fires somewhere in the region—we aren't too sure where—to flare-up and start pouring out more smoke and ash

> '...there is still panic. Being on high alert 24/7 is proving taxing on us all, and many within the centre have already lost their homes.'

again. With people already expecting the worst, this triggers the fire plan we had all been informed of at dinner the night before. Women are filling saucepans with water and placing them around the cabin verandas. Outdoor spas are filled with water. There is high activity with the men and some of the boys running around with hoses desperately attempting to wet-down walls, walkways, rooves and whatever is exposed.

As informed as we all are, there is still panic. Being on high alert 24/7 is proving taxing on us all, and many within the centre have already lost their homes. They know what the fire can do. Children are underfoot, unsure and insecure, seeing all the big people rushing about. One youngish mum in a cabin nearby is screaming for everyone to, 'grab a f*ing hose and save the place, the fire's on its way'.

Not long after her outburst, a guy drives through the park like a bat-out-of-hell, barely missing some adults and kids as he hoons past. Jerking to a halt, he jumps out of his car and begins swearing and shouting that the entire Bay Ridge area is now burning out of control. For a few minutes he is inconsolable and threatening to jump back in his car and head over to the north side of the Bay where he imagines the fire to be burning. He has been drinking heavily and is in no position to drive anywhere. Step quickly approaches the poor guy and points out that the smoke he can see in the distance is, in fact, nowhere near the Bay Ridge area, but much further north and to the west of there. Thankfully, he is still open to reason, a hug, and a soothing, 'It's alright mate, it's a simple mistake, no need to worry'.

The fires have posed a potential threat to the Bay Ridge area on a few occasions over the past month, leaving me again concerned about our new church, as it's situated in this new subdivision to the north of the bridge. If the wind does swing around to the north, we could be in big trouble.

Southland has been operating in the local area for 33 years, but until recently we hadn't had a place to call our own. With much sweat and effort over a couple of years we finally built a beautiful new building called the Olive Tree. This modern and well-equipped facility is where Southland meets each Sunday, and is also readily available as a community space for anyone who needs it. The thought of losing the building, on top of everything else that's happened, is not something I want to deal with. But right now, it appears to be safe.

We keep a concerned eye on a large plume of smoke rising from an area directly north-west of town. With the winds coming predominantly from an easterly direction, we haven't been too worried about this fire front, but all of a sudden, the smoke starts to lean menacingly towards us, which can only mean the wind has swung around to the north. This is exactly what we don't want to happen! If the wind doesn't change, and very soon, Bay Ridge and Surfside are really in for it!

All along the southern bank of the Clyde River (the safe side), we gather to watch this potential disaster as it unfolds before us. People are muttering and mumbling to themselves and shaking their heads in horror and disbelief as the fire looks to be advancing rapidly towards Bay Ridge and Surfside. Our concern is that a strong southerly wind is predicted later in the afternoon, and if fires manage to get across the Princes Highway and ignite Surfside, there is nothing to stop them burning all the way to North Durras. This will lead to the total destruction of Surfside, our town of Long Beach, Maloneys Beach, South Durras, and what remains of Murramarang National Park. North of that, the fires have already ravaged the towns on December 4 and again on December 6.

As I stand and watch, I overhear a bystander talking on the phone to a friend, declaring that 'Surfside is well and truly going, you gotta get out now!' Panicked rumours continue hourly, as people attempt to interpret what we are going through. I am horrified at the thought of what might happen if the wind doesn't change within the next 10 or 15 minutes.

Things are not looking good. We need a miraculous downpour of rain. We need the wind to change. We need to be anywhere else, doing anything else. It is torture—standing with bated breath wondering if we are about to see our homes go up in smoke, or worried about the embers burning the cabins we are meant to be feeling 'safe' in.

When we were up in Long Beach, we often didn't know where the fires were. But here— watching flames leap over the mountains, every now and again seeing huge plumes of polluted, black smoke rise as another building is taken—this is madness. Everyone is on edge. We truly do not know what is going to happen next.

People are sitting in cars, ready to drive them into the water! Hoses are still being sprayed over our cabins; yet everyone else is watching the flames. We are attempting to fake a calm for the sake of the kiddies but it is bleedingly obvious there is no calm here. Nobody can tear their eyes away from the mountains. All our faces are upturned toward the sky and the hills and the smoke and flames; as though being able to watch it come will ignite an escape plan. Every word uttered is about the fire. Nothing exists outside of this infernal moment. Time stands still. Some are holding hands, others have cigarettes and wine in their hands; most just stare, speechless.

During this torturous time, my youngest daughter made a sensible decision on behalf of the children.

Jordan

It had all been getting too much for the kids. They had seen and heard enough manic panic. I grabbed my sister Kelita and her children, and we took them all down to the swimming pool and watched them laugh and play freely. Kelita and I kept one eye on the sky as it turned dark red and was filled with the smoke and flames of the not-too-distant fires.

There was no denying that all the adults were scared. I was scared. It looked like the fire was coming right at us. A lot of my fear was that my children would be experiencing fear. Then I remember looking in the pool and being so relieved, as a parent, to see my kids playing innocently, almost carefree. It had been a great plan to get them away from the hype.

I mean, I've seen my kids scared back when it was just smoke. Yet then, even as their Dad was within sight, hosing down cabins and trees against potential spot-fires; as the entire heavy, sky turned dark red, and I was thinking, if there ever is a time to be stressed, this would be it, my children were just playing with their cousins like we were all on a great big holiday together.

From the fireground—January 4, 2020

And then we get our miracle. As I watch in the forefront of the crowd—praying under my breath—the breeze starts to swing around and blow from behind us, from the south! Before I can think about what is happening, the smoke column from the nearby fire begins to head in the opposite direction—away from town, away from Surfside, and thankfully, away from my new home at Long Beach.

Shock. That's the word. We are all in shock. At first, we stand stunned, together. Nobody knows what the right words or actions for this situation can be. Men are still wielding hoses. Cigarettes are still being chain-smoked.

And then, we begin a hug-fest. That powerful universal, non-verbal connection that says all the words we can't find to express. Everyone exhales, collectively. We can breathe. We all start cheering, carrying on a treat. The kiddies, back from the pool, are spellbound watching the adults change mood so quickly, and we grab them and begin dancing, telling them everything is going to be alright. We want to yell from the rooftops that we are alive and we are safe. Again. Nobody wants to add, 'for now'.

Hottest place on earth

That evening and the following few days, things remained pretty hectic around about us. Though it was all quiet on the home front where we were evacuated together, we were reminded that the rescue workers were having no such reprieve. All through the daylight hours we listened to sirens. Out on Beach Road, fire trucks, SES vehicles, police and ambos head here, there, and everywhere. We didn't even bat an eye now at the sight of what once were novelties—the fire-bombing planes and the choppers with the big water-ball dangling precariously beneath them, scooping from the river in front of us and heading back toward the thick of the fires. It still felt like a warzone but there seemed to have been a subtle shift over the past few days from an 'every-man-for-themselves' attitude, to a 'let's pull together and do what we can to help everyone get through this'.

During this time Australia was recorded as the hottest place on earth! NSW seemed like one giant melting pot that nothing could survive. Penrith had recorded the highest ever temperature for the Sydney Basin at 48.9 degrees.

On January 5 there were nine fires at emergency level and 12 at 'watch and act', with temperatures in their 40s in Batemans Bay and recorded winds up to 104 kilometres per hour. Our capital city recorded 43 degrees and Nowra was at 40.6 degrees.

'The smoke was still with us and just wouldn't let up. I was so sick of it some days I could have screamed.'

Things were out of control. I wondered how we hadn't lost more lives with the winds, the high temperatures, the unpredictability and lack of manpower to fight against such conditions, knowing there were 150 bushfires continuing to burn throughout our State. The bushfire crisis was having a devastating impact not only on individuals, but whole communities, the businesses, our beautiful environment and Australia's flora and fauna. It was difficult to see a way forward.

The smoke was still with us and just wouldn't let up. I was so sick of it some days I could have screamed (except it would have hurt my throat). Everyone had sore eyes, scratchy throats, and nagging little coughs that weren't enough to be a big concern, but just enough to be a nuisance—including all the wee ones. I felt sorry for our beautiful babies, who were all irritated with what the smoke was doing to their lungs, eyes and throats but were unable to express themselves other than rubbing at their red eyes and noses.

Again than night, Kelita and Jordan washed towers of dishes and pans after feeding the firies and all the evacuees—all done by candlelight with cold water, by hand. If it wasn't for the constant trauma, you could say we are 'glamping'. It could almost be fun if not for the reality of fires, living under constant threat, family without a home to go to and the huge clean-up tasks ahead. Sigh.

We'd been at the evac centre a few days beyond the second wave of fires to do what we could and to stay safe. Regular updates came through to Kellie and the staff, who were able to keep us semi-informed, and we had more spurts of phone access, so we didn't feel as isolated as we'd been in Long Beach.

Those of us with homes to go back to had no power, and therefore no water and were without communication, so we were encouraged to stay longer at the Coachhouse. Mum was holding up better with a room of her own in Ben's cabin, to often slip away to, and my daughters had their babies to care for, so it made sense to stay where water—even freezing cold— was available. We needed a safe, secure and semi-comfortable environment to keep life rolling along with some sort of normality.

What was normality? Everywhere was in disarray. Nothing was as it should be. And though I tried hard during that time to imagine the calm and 'ordinary' lifestyles others were enjoying in other places in the country, my messy and all-consuming here-and-now totally obliterated any ideas of utopia!

One thing that helped get things in perspective was Sunday. I love Sundays. And this Sunday was to be no different—I would end up loving it despite what was going on around us. Admittedly, we were all a little shaken, having miraculously survived the next round of fires, but nothing would get in the way of bringing in the New Year with praise. Most of us were able to be at a church service we held that first Sunday morning of 2020, in the dark, in the foyer of the Olive Tree, with acoustic guitars to sing along to. We raised our voices high with praises. The catastrophic predictions had been wrong. Long Beach had been spared. There in that very special service, grace and peace were the two words Father had given me to carry through 2020. I had the privilege of sharing this around Communion during our humble little church service. Grace and Peace be with us all.

CHAPTER 7

Penning a poem or three

I don't think we can underestimate the impact of social media during the worst of the fire season. There has been a lot of negative feedback about some aspects of social media, more broadly in the past, and it has been good to see the 'powers that be' make changes and attempt to address issues. I have to say though, that Facebook, Messenger and Instagram (my preferred channels) opened the door to a wealth of support for so many of us. Each post brought encouragement, the trolls seemed to have gone back under the bridges they came from and people were championing one another.

Throughout most of the ordeal, I posted regularly on social media—initially to keep friends and extended family members updated, because most forms of communication were poor. Also, there were so many individual messages to deal with that having one 'post' worked for all of us. It also proved a cathartic exercise for me, becoming a bit of a rambling journal that I looked forward to continuing each day. It brought me comfort, and the encouragement I received from others served as much as a soothing balm to me as I was to them.

Many times, I was using my words and photos in an attempt to either process the days happenings or prepare myself for what was to come.

My friend Cathy posted her brother's heartfelt poem on Facebook just a week after he lost his home to the fires. His mother Lyn told me that his poem had come 'straight from his heart.' Jim and I met up over lunch at JJ's on the Marina in the centre of town, not far from where I had been evacuated to—

and not that far from where Jim's home had been swallowed by the fire, right before his eyes.

Jim

The Burning Bay poem just sprung out of me. I've been thinking in rhyme ever since and have written another 20 poems since that first one. Even as we're sitting here, I have to stop myself from making everything rhyme.

I've been in the Bay for 25 years—long enough to have met, married and divorced—there's a lotta things you can do in the Bay, ha-ha.

I fought my bloody hardest to save our family home, built in 1968, but just had to give up the fight. There was no winning against that fire! On that New Year's Eve morning, me and a few mates fought against the fire there at Catalina until the ground became so hot it melted the souls of my steel-capped sneakers. It was that hot! I watched mulch in the gardens around me, just spring up into flames. Spot fires were breaking out everywhere. And then the fire front hit and I knew there was no saving the house.

Even as that first water tanker pulled up, it was already too late for anyone to do anything. I had to get out of the heat so I went across the road and filmed my house burning until my mobile phone got so hot in my hand that it just crapped itself and stopped working.

After that I wandered around in a daze, barefooted, wearing nothing but the shorts and singlet I had been wearing under my other clothes while I fought the fire. I had thrown my dirty, stinking jeans and melted sneakers in the bin, not realising I might need them. I wasn't thinking straight, my brain was totally numb.

When it first happened, I wandered into town, only to discover everything was closed, or closing. The power was out everywhere. I went past the Bayview Pub and the owner stuck his head out and asked, 'Are you alright, Jim?' I told him, 'My house just burnt down'.

He was about to lock up, but he suggested I come in and have a beer with him. I told him, 'If it isn't too rude, I'd love a six-pack,' and he just handed me a case. I didn't know what else to do, so I took it up to a mate's house.

That first week, not being able to go home, I kind of wondered where I fit in the warzone that was my neighbourhood, where another six homes close to mine were destroyed that same day.

I think I was 'walking round in circles' for at least the first few days. It took me a week to even get a pair of shoes. I didn't eat for days, either. When the power came on for a day there, in-between all the blackouts, Coles opened, but the queues were two to three hours long. I just wanted a bread roll or something.

I went over to the Reject Shop and grabbed soap, a toothbrush, toothpaste and one clean shirt. When I went to pay for it the girl just gave it to me, she wouldn't take any money. After that someone sent me to the Hanging Rock Evacuation Centre. I didn't want to be a nuisance to anyone or impose on anyone. I just went without at first because I wasn't used to accepting charity.

I didn't have much choice in the matter though, and from then on I was given clothes, bedding and all sorts of stuff from friends and family all over the State.

I also grabbed some stuff from the Resource Centre at Mackay Park that the army were manning. My 11-year-old daughter, Raeden likes UP&GO, so I got her three of them. I picked up a couple of things for myself and put them in the car. I couldn't think beyond the moment and I had no idea what I needed, so I filled my hands and went to leave. Before I could drive away, one of the Army Reserve volunteers came over to chat with me at the car. After talking for a bit, I took off back to where I was staying. It was only when I go there that I realised that, while we had been chatting, other Reservists had been filling my car with all sorts of goodies without me even knowing what was going on. As I began to get the stuff out of the car, instead of three UP&GO, there were three boxes! And they'd done the same with everything else. I've always earned my own way, so thinking of myself as a 'charity case' kind of rubbed me the wrong way.

It was there, at that make-shift Resource Centre that sprung up and hung around for about a month, that I shared my poem with one of the guys. I read *The Burning Bay* to him and he was really moved. He asked me if he could keep the copy of it and read it to the boys at mess. When he read it, the Army boys fell to pieces. One of them grabbed a heap of cardboard and wrote the whole thing out and stuck it up at the centre. Everybody knew about it after that. And my sister's Facebook post has already received about 10,000 likes. It was through this, as word got out among old mates, that I started reconnecting with them. Everyone told me I needed to be on social media—turns out I'd missed a reunion or two, which was a bit of a shame. So, believe it or not, I'm on Facebook now.

So here's the infamous poem that is now being shared around the world. I recited it on radio (https://soundcloud.com/user-700728214) when I was interviewed by ABC South East Coast reporter Daniel Doody. He's a good bloke and reckoned I should get it published. I've got so many poems now, I wouldn't mind putting together a book of 'em.

The Burning Bay

Jim Hughes, January 7, 2020
Where fires are burning for over a month and a day
I live on the coast, in sunny Batemans Bay.
It's still going on with no end in sight
There's no other choice but to stand up and fight.
I've had my bloody turn, it came on in a hurry
We did the best we could, there was no time to worry.
It was Roger, Dad and Me, there was Chriso and Mark
Everyone else had left before the first spark.

We'll be alright, we'll give it a crack
We did our absolute best, we thought we'd beaten it back.
Then up through the gully came the wind and the roar
We lost water pressure, we couldn't do more.
The smoke and the heat was driving us just barmy
It would have been great to have a big bloody army.
Time to get out, enough time to run
Jump in the car, smoke's blocked out the sun.
I stopped on the corner, filmed my house burn to the ground
The heat and the smoke had battered us round.
Mine couldn't be saved when I saw the first tanker
You bloody firebugs and looters, your name rhymes
with banker.
To know where I live, it was a quiet little street
Now six of us are gone, the damage complete.
With services down, the power's gone out
Todd still has cold beer, it's his bloody shout.
Now there's the stories of what's gone around
It's not just us here, its damn near destroyed towns.
Mogo is damaged, Cobargo's almost not there
Rosedale is in ashes, but us resilient people still care.
It's not just the people or property lost
The poor bloody creatures, consider their cost.
From animals on land, even ones in the rivers and sea
The smoke and the ash, it's devastating me!
So put your hose down, turn your tap off
Flush every third, put up with the 'whaff'.
Then there's the firies, the boots on the ground
Doin' their absolute best, but stretched all around.
The volunteers everywhere trying to do their best,
All at the evac centres, they'll lift your spirits like a
welcome guest.
I have my family and friends, just so much support
My daughter, my angel, she's my trooper a real sport.
The only house my girl's ever known, just burned to

the ground

She misses her teddy, he's just not around.

I'm not looking for sympathy, I want none of that here,

We could meet at the Bayview for an icy cold beer.

If you read my little story, from near or from far

There's always some way to help, wherever you are.

Our agencies who care, Red Cross, Anglicare and the

RF bloody S

You all can donate, just think bloody YES!!

So if you think you can help, even in any small way

It's the whole eastern seaboard, not just our

beautiful 'Burning Bay'.

My poem has sparked a lot of attention since my sister whacked it on Facebook, which encouraged me to write more—about the firefighters and the pilots who flew the water bombers. I don't know where these poems come from, but they've really helped me through this. I've got seven really good mates who have lost all they had and they reckon the poems are beauties. I try to read them to the family but they're in tears by half-way through. Mum's in tears, my daughter's bawling, and even the mates tear-up when I read them.

With *The Burning Bay* poem going round the world, my daughter has been receiving teddy-bears every day. They just turn up on her doorstep, sometimes with little notes. I call her 'The Teddy Bear Girl' now. They just keep coming.

Even though we're keen to rebuild, it's a long journey before we can think about moving back home. We just started renting a nice, local place that we hope we'll be able to stay in for the long-haul. Raeden couldn't even go back to our block for some time to have a look. For the first week, it was too much for her. She couldn't bear to see it. About two weeks after it burned, she was ready—and that's when she told me she wanted us to rebuild. I thought it was a great idea. I was happy with that. I thought that if we could busy ourselves with the new house plans it would keep our minds off the damn fires.

With the plans all done now, we're hoping by the time Council clears our block, we'll have approval to go ahead and we can get cracking.

As we were looking around the ruins of our home, we found some of the old, pressed tin roof. It was all twisted and bent out of shape but my daughter wants to keep it and use it as artwork in the new place. I had to laugh. Raeden is into calligraphy and because she likes my first poem so much she wants to write it out all fancy and put it on the wall. I'm happy to let her do that.

It also keeps us talking about the future and looking forward to starting again—something we both need to do.

While talking with Jim, my mind had occasionally drifted to Kelita, whose home burnt down not long after Jim's that day, just up the road from his. Jim showed me the video he'd recorded on his phone, and he had filmed the fire 'jumping' across the road and roaring up the gully that runs behind my daughter's home. It was very confronting—watching live fire destroy so much that was precious to our family and community. There was one point where the two of us just sat for a while, as though we were reserving a minute's silence for all the Catalina residents, and beyond.

Jim wrote that first poem on January 7, the day after the highway heading north was finally re-opened. Speed-limits had been greatly reduced and travellers were advised to take precaution as trees were still precariously placed along the roadside, with authorities unsure how many were yet to fall. My 81-year-old Mum, who had taken everything in her stride— the threats, the thick smoke, the evacuations, the cold showers, no contact with the outside world, helping comfort the littlies as needed—had been with us since before Christmas and was ready to go home. Once the roads were opened, it was time to head the 189 kilometres north. I felt relieved for her, but sad

'Though I would never have wanted
my Mum to endure as much as we did
during that Christmas "festive" season,
nevertheless, on so many levels, I was
glad she was with us.'

for us. She had been a huge help, and often the reason I was able to stay strong when I needed to. But it was my brother's birthday and Mum was keen to see him. She would have been exhausted, let's face it, but she wasn't going to let on while she was with us. She was a calming force for everyone. The littlies were thrilled to have 'Great Nan' with us wherever we went; it added to that holiday feel we hoped the kids were falling for.

Though I would never have wanted my Mum to endure as much as we did during that Christmas 'festive' season, nevertheless, on so many levels, I was glad she was with us. We are family and we were together.

Though I set my mind on staying strong to celebrate every tiny victory that presented itself, it was difficult to say goodbye to Mum. I remember driving her down to a familiar part within town so she could steer her little blue car, which was now covered in dirt and dust and ash, toward home. When I got out to hand over the reins so to speak, I could hardly speak. It had been awesome having Mum here, but it was so good to see her be able to escape, to head to freedom where the air was clear and her home was a safe-haven and she had no fear of being rushed out in the middle of the night. I was so happy for her, but waving goodbye was very difficult. I was glad of the walk back to the Coachhouse where it was time to prepare myself for whatever was to come next.

By then, they had managed to bring a little more order to things back at the evac centre. Teams had been set up, assigned to each need. Food, clothes, medical, water, toys, books, bedding—things were taking shape and being run well. After Mum left, I went back up there to register Step and my extended stay. I could tell there was too much to store and sort. It was getting difficult to move around up there. I figured it wouldn't be long before things were moved to a larger venue, nevertheless I was surprised with everyone's kindness and patience despite being very tired, all facing their own trauma and being stuck in a hot, stuffy room with many confused and dazed customers to deal with. I look back with fond affection, believing that experiencing the empathy and assistance within the evac centre, with Red Cross and Anglicare workers pouring love all over us, was crucial to people's well-being at the time.

My big-hearted, always-serving, friend Helen, is a trained care-worker and a member of both the Country Women's Association and Anglicare. Batemans Bay CWA raised money and were given donations for local use and provided vouchers for shopping for each family that was submitted by members.

The evac centre was Government-run to help with emergency accommodation. Agencies like Anglicare, Red Cross and Salvation Army volunteers were there for the people. It was Anglicare's job to deal with personal needs like toothbrushes, toothpaste, brushes, shampoo and conditioner, soap, sanitary items, razors, nappies, formula and baby food through to underwear, clothing and footwear.

As time went on, they were able to help with all types of food, bedding, shopping vouchers, mobile phones and generators, also assisting with emotional support and helping with animal and pet needs. The Salvation Army had the huge job of supplying three meals a day, plus morning and afternoon teas and even supper for all the people that had registered as evacuees.

The largest meal supplied was for 2,500 misplaced people. The Indian Community and Kohli's restaurant cooked and fed the entire evacuation centre on two occasions and Golden Lake Chinese supplied a dinner banquet. The entire community has been great.

School holidays at last

I guess the first day for our crew to experience anything closely resembling school holidays was Thursday, January 9. Because the other days were so weird, doing something ordinary meant we experienced a very different day. While Kelita went to the real estate agencies looking for accommodation, I took four of my grandies to the movies and we enjoyed a long-awaited, well-needed, laugh watching *My Spy* at the local cinema. This too, had been closed for so long and was only then able to open its doors to screen movies. I'm guessing the staff had rigged up some generators, but it's possible that by then this area of town had power back on. Anyway, to celebrate it being open, tickets were just $10, so we were there with bells on, munching from a too-large box of popcorn and licking choc-top ice-creams. I loved watching joy return to the children. Thank you, Perry Street Cinemas, just one of the many local businesses who created incentives to restore a holiday feel and generously give to the community.

It was also 'ordinary' for Step and I in the fact that we returned to our bush Love Shack the night before. There hadn't been many nights in the Love Shack since we'd moved in during December—what with fires and stand-by alerts. It felt nice to sleep in our own bed, though it was nothing more than a borrowed mattress on the floor. We knew that a further warning for Long Beach had been predicted for the weekend. We were making the most of the calm before the storm, so to speak.

Kelita and her family remained at the Coachhouse, having extended their stay by another four days until they could figure out what came next. Beautiful friends from Canberra, Norm and Sue Fraser, had offered their holiday home to them and they were overcome with their generosity. They didn't want to rush anywhere until they got their bearings on what the future may look like for their little tribe. They'd been to four different temporary dwellings since their home burnt down and they needed some sort of stability while ever it was available.

The rest of us knew it was likely that we would all be back again sooner rather than later as predicted fires and winds were expected to worsen. It seemed endless, but we were ever hopeful that someday soon, this would pass.

Rampant generosity

As a community, we were enduring well. Generosity was rampant with people offering anything they had to anyone who needed it. If we hadn't remained in that 'high alert' state, I am sure there would have been so much joy and happiness and celebrating all around. But there wasn't the energy or the inkling while the air remained thick with smoke and fires remained out of control. Still, we were so grateful. There were always those incredible, inspiring little stories amidst the heartbreak and loss. I believe our town will continue to be kind after this traumatic time; I think we have embraced that 'tribe vibe' where we can see ourselves as 'one'. We are pulling together as one people through this trauma and will rebuild out the other side of it, emerging stronger, closer and a more compassionate community.

I see God's hand at work everywhere. That compassionate heart that will give and keep on giving, love and keep on loving, serve and keep on serving. Personal agendas on hold, people focusing on others. Giving without expectation of returns. That's not often normal human-nature but this experience has shone such a light on goodness and kindness that I honestly think there will be so many experiencing 'mystery' blessings for quite some time. In God's economy, you can't out-give Him. He always gives back, sometimes tenfold, other times one-hundred-times what was given. There will be immeasurable rewards gained and gleaned—lessons, friendships and blessings—that no money could ever buy.

Meanwhile, I kept the day rolling along as though it were an ordinary day. After our movie and dropping the kiddies off to their parents, I did some washing at the cabin and picked up a mirror for the Love Shack from my friend Trish, who had recently moved house. This was followed by a very hot afternoon delivering supplies. The day got hotter and hotter as the hours ticked by and driving around in Buzz, without air-conditioning, I ended-up a slippery ball of sweat. I couldn't wait to get to our Love Shack and our swimming pool.

Evacuating again

As I walked in the door, Step informed me that we would be evacuating again the next day as conditions had gradually worsened. Nobody knew what the next day might bring. While in town earlier, I had watched Army trucks and choppers and strike teams arriving en masse so I thought, 'whatever comes, we're as ready as we can be.'

On Friday January 10, I could have been excused for wondering, 'Will this ever end?' It seemed the fires were continuously one step ahead of us all. In the past, when we had prepared for it to hit in the afternoon, it had ravaged our towns early in the morning. This time, as we prepared for it to hit tomorrow, it blew through on high winds in the middle of the night.

I knew we had to stay strong, but when the evacuated are preparing to evacuate the evacuation centre, it is permissible to wonder! Surviving yet another hairy night of high anxiety for some (as nerves are frayed) as a destructive southerly whipped through the coast, is to be celebrated. Though it was mostly wind and smoke and red skies for our crew, nobody knew when and where another fire would flare. The air was often alive with burning embers amidst the thick smoke.

The winds truly were insane. For Kelita at the Coachhouse evac centre, things went more than a little wild.

Kelita

The sky was lit up with red. My heart was racing. My hubby was preparing to evacuate and people here were evacuating.

We had sirens blaring, winds ripping through and the smoke covering the sky again. We think a fire had been deliberately lit down near the beach, but nobody knows. It is just so exhausting being under attack again and again. Each time we think we can relax or that we're safe, it comes back and we wonder whether it will ever end.

'Not again!' seemed to be my first thought as each of these flaming waves crashed over our town. We faced destruction on every road, north or south. Our once leafy, beautiful, relaxing drives through our beautiful coastland were now painful, gut-wrenching and heartbreaking. It was *difficult*, and remains so. Reality slips in and it isn't pretty. And all the while, there was the constant uncertainty. There wasn't anyone telling us, 'It's okay, it will be over soon.' If only we could have heard those words early in January, but in fact we were not to hear those words for another month, and that was part of the exhaustion, part of the reason why nobody was able to relax. We were on edge, living in a warzone where the 'enemy' could strike at any moment from any position.

We felt so precariously vulnerable—but for the strength, love, resilience and generosity of people! Supplies and helpers were arriving and our local crews worked around the clock. We saw teams of people helping. The locals were hugging, linking arms, looking up, trusting God, sharing tears, embracing the loss and believing for reprieve. Strangers have become friends. Strangers from afar have become our heroes as they fought fires, got supplies through and poured generosity and compassion upon us. Local businesses and clubs and teams did everything within their power to assist.

Once again, our family was safe, our homes were being fire-prepped again, and our mission to help others shine their light, continued.

It was Ben's birthday, Saturday, January 11. We attempted

to make it a day of continuous celebrations over this amazing human even though celebrating almost seemed wrong under the circumstances we were all facing. The party had been postponed twice due to heat, fire danger, ash, low spirits, being unable to shop and the list went on.

Eventually it was a fun, well-needed get-together of games, swimming in the pool, eating too much party food and having the little children running around dripping water off their goose-bumped bodies. There was laughter in the air, candles, a cake and even a piñata. The sky remained ominous and the air was thick with threat, but we partied anyway. It was my son's 38th birthday.

I'd had a busy morning of distractions from the fires. I'd helped raise funds for our brigade with some local friends and a couple of visiting guys, simply by enjoying a delicious almond chai and listening to Mark Smith's live music with the overly-generous Kylie and Jess at Tribe Cafe. I'd considered it a welcome reprieve but my friend Angela, who had joined us with her daughter Alexandra, said that it had been more than that, 'So good to meet these amazing humans visiting our community purely to share, support and uplift—both a privilege and an honour.'

It was inspirational meeting so many who were doing their bit in whatever way they could find to help. I was out delivering groceries and clothing in Buzz again for a few hours after the café, stopping in on those who were holed-up in motel rooms until they were found better accommodation and hugs were shared and tears were shed everywhere. Stories told... so many stories! The Aussie spirit rocks! We may get knocked down, but we were certainly planning on getting up again, and stronger than ever!

And then it was Sunday again, the second Sunday of January (the 12th) 2020. We had survived another week.

Just watch the children

When in doubt, just watch the children—these beautiful pure-hearted granddaughters of mine, Mia, Willow and Chili were continually creating ways to give, asking who next they could do something special for. Under Sylvia's guidance, they had painted some rocks with cute pictures and happy sayings and had set up a little stall after church to raise funds to give to the real heroes, our local volunteer firies. They did this off their own bat—that's what makes some of these things so special, that there is such a strong sense of community happening that the little children are picking up on it and finding creative ways to get involved.

They weren't the only children giving resources, time and talent to help others. Recently I humbly received a gift of a much-loved football from an 11-year-old 'camped' at the evac centre, who was so excited to give it to me when he heard Harper had lost his in the fire. Another two young children of friends of ours in Murwillumbah, Clara and Sonny, saved up their pocket money and deposited it into our daughter's account to get something for her children, as did Isaac, another young person in Queensland. These are but a few stories of the many that will be told and retold as time goes on.

Coachhouse manager Kellie, in making her resort a safe haven for evacuees, was run off her feet. She is well able to be proud of her two young girls who served tirelessly at every turn. Children—their hearts are pure, seeing needs and *enjoying* finding ways to fulfil them. A stall of rocks and home-baked treats from my little, mighty warriors-of-light, making sure people have toilet paper, finding a way to amuse littlies when the parents are pre-occupied, making-up songs to deal with their trauma and teaching them to others—the children amazed me.

I know everyone has a story, a story it is important for them to be able to share, but the ones about the little children leading the way, they're my favourites.

"'I'll take you home to bed." It seemed such a simple statement. His eyes opened wide and he replied, "But our house is burnt down.'"

CHAPTER 8
Let the children come

Let's take a break from the January timeline for a few chapters and reflect from a number of perspectives on how this disaster has impacted all our children and also what we can learn from them and this experience.

While we were all in the Coachhouse, I remember one night when H was so exhausted, he fell asleep on the lounge in one of the cabins. While there, curled into a ball, it was heartbreaking watching him twitch and call out, distressed in his sleep. It was obvious that his six-year-old brain was racing through way more images than his little body could handle. Eventually Kelita came in and tried to pick him up, gently assuring him things were okay, 'Come on, Mate.'

H semi woke-up, and as he looked up at his Mummy he asked, 'Where are we going?'

Kelita stroked his hair and said, 'I'll take you home to bed.' It seemed such a simple statement. His eyes opened wide and he replied, 'But our house is burnt down.'

Another incident that comes to mind occurred while the kids were all playing during one of the spells where the fire situation seemed to have temporarily calmed down. Some of the families had decided to leave the evacuation centre and head home to begin the inevitable clean ups. One of my older grandchildren said, 'We're going home today.' H looked at the other children, all getting ready to leave the Coachhouse and, hanging his head, said, 'I'm not. My house burnt down.'

There were many similar innocent incidences where we realised that his young mind was attempting to grasp his present

'While grief is a strange thing, and everyone moves through it differently, it does have an important purpose in that it helps us adjust our thinking and our perspective on life...'

future stability in the midst of losing everything familiar to him. And this challenge continues for him—six weeks after he lost everything, he underwent his first counselling session.

One thing I have noticed is that his love for Lego and models has greatly increased. As he follows instructions and figures out where things go, his problem-solving skills are honed, and this is helping him to take control over some of the stresses.

The purpose of grief

As I mentioned, of my 14 grandchildren, only three were away from the fires when they hit in successive waves from New Year's Eve and on through January. That left 11 of them going through this—with us supporting them all in the best ways we could. The three, Harper, London and Lennox, who lost their home in the big one, showed our family that we had to 'circle the wagons' and help them recover as best as possible. While grief is a strange thing, and everyone moves through it differently, it does have an important purpose in that it helps us adjust our thinking and our perspective on life in relation to the things we experience and encounter.

We weren't about to ignore grief or sweep it aside like it was an unwanted inconvenience. The first thing we knew we had to do was to continuously gather as family so that unconditional love and affection could be poured onto and into them. As our little ones were faced with a situation that threatened their security and shook their reality, they needed to be reassured that they were still going to be loved-on and nurtured and

On the day Kelita and her family's home burnt down, she and her husband picked up their house number from the burnt remains of their letterbox and said, 'This is all we have left of our house.'

Top: A blood red sky near Tomakin.

Below: The author while evacuated to the Coachhouse, washing up after a dinner for evacuees and firefighters.

Top: Kelita and children Harper, London and Lennox survey what is left of their home.
Below: Kelita's family home burning at about 1.30pm on December 31, 2019.

'The fires have changed us, but as we look around,
we see green shoots everywhere.' *Page 178*

protected. Under the circumstances we faced and they continue to face, this is where the love of our close and connected family truly shines, as we work our healing magic in the hearts and minds of our grandies.

When Kelita and her family had first arrived at the Coachhouse, they had that hollowed-out look that often accompanies grief or trauma. We made a point of spending as much time together as we could, doing what we always do—sharing meals, playing games together, and trying to keep the atmosphere relatively positive and optimistic. Not wanting to suppress or deny our feelings, we also made space for anyone needing to express their fears and concerns around the fires and what was happening around us.

Kelita's children had experienced many difficult moments. London and Lennox were showing slight signs of trauma and we all felt for H. As young children, they had gone through so much. H went from feeling like he was going to burn to death stuck in the fire, to almost suffocating in their caravan in the most intense heat a body could stand. These kids saw their home full of flames, had watched the video of it later, and had returned when it was mere rubble.

H wanted to watch the video over and over, to keep visualising it, for the first week. He wanted to go back and look at what was once his home. Kelita and her hubby took the kids up to the block and let them look around, cry, talk through what they were thinking and feeling. Ever the optimist, as they were leaving, H said, 'Don't worry, Mummy, in our next house we can have a bath and a pool.'

I think it was then they knew they just couldn't go back there. The stench of smoke would make Kelita's hubby angry as he too was being haunted by the memories of the house in flames. They decided they didn't want to try to rebuild what they had there.

Back at the Coachhouse, we encouraged the kids to play games together outdoors where natural energy is more abundant.

Step was really good at this; he loves outdoors and didn't like the constant chatter about the fires, so was often calling for the kiddies to go and explore with him. This was a wonderful opportunity for them to escape into a fantasy world where the make-believe of childhood could come alive through waterplay, building sandcastles and inventing magic kingdoms. We didn't have power at the evac centre, so it meant the kids weren't glued to electronic devices or watching television—which was a very good thing, from what we've heard, it had been constant footage of fires. We didn't want the kids wallowing inside for extended periods. It was our aim to provide a positive environment for them, allowing the healing and recovery process plenty of space.

In all the chaos and uncertainty, many people admitted later that there was a relaxed kind of enjoyment during the time when we had no power. It took us back to a simpler kind of life. During the day, our grandies played soccer, football, rode bikes and scooters, splashed in the pool and every so often went off on their little adventures with their Pa. A real winner was exploring the nearby sandflats at low tide where thousands of soldier crabs prompted many a laugh and squeal of delight. We also stumbled upon a blue-ringed octopus in a shallow rock pool, which added another level of excitement to the day.

Being together in one place gave the kids that vital sense of sameness and security they were accustomed to before the fires and needed more than ever. This was good for them in developing positive relationships and learning how to understand and cope with their fears and anxieties together. We were able to address sadness, anger or aggression and build empathy within them all. We continuously helped them build their self-esteem through praise and helping them change their 'I can't' into 'I believe I can' statements. We also reminded them to make good use of the everyday things they use to comfort themselves.

They had all brought items that were dear to them, so we encouraged extra use of them if they needed it. Where we could, we surrounded our kids with their favourite toys, stuffed animals, and much-loved books and even some movies that Mace managed to set up on some fandangle device of his. We didn't deprive them of these things or impose ridiculous rules on the older ones who were showing signs of regressive behaviour after trauma, we knew this to be quite normal. Actually, I was impressed observing them comfort themselves and be able to self-calm during some of the scary times.

London and H kept busy with all their new toys, gathering more and more each day as donations came flooding in from people all over the place—friends and strangers alike.

Lauren

I'm so grateful we could gather as a family at Coachhouse. For days before we left for there, I was having dreams of needing to evacuate quickly and not being able to get to my baby. There'd been days without power, so I guess the dark nights with our baby in another room had affected me. I was relieved when we finally left and I could set things up as best we could at the Coachhouse. I was really keen to attempt to keep some form of normalcy for him.

During our evacuation, after days of thinking about preparing our property, it still felt like we did everything at the last minute, like we weren't quite prepared, no matter what we did. It's all good to have a fire plan in theory, but putting it into practice is such a huge thing. We were both nervous about having to leave our home because we hadn't been in it long and had only just settled in before we were figuring out what to leave behind. By then though, Ben and I knew we had no choice but to evacuate; everybody expected the fires to sweep through Long Beach and we just weren't equipped to fight them. After all we'd seen and heard about the New Year's Eve fires, we were suddenly taking things very seriously.

I think some of the hardest things to deal with during the weeks surrounding New Year's Eve and beyond was the constant 'unknown'. It was so frustrating not knowing where was safe and the continuous lack of communication impacted me greatly. Not being able to communicate with my parents was hard. Their home is in Ulladulla, which had its own fire threats and embers were falling in their yard, too. When you're in these situations, you really want to be able to stay in touch with those you love, you need that peace of mind. We weren't able to have that.

And when you have a baby to care for, things look very different. There's so much you need to have with you to tend to the needs of your child. I needed bottles, a way to store my breastmilk in a cold space and somewhere I could then warm it to feed River—not to mention packing his cot, his bumbo chair and the pram. He sleeps with a comforter rug we call 'baby' and has a dummy—so I needed to make sure they were on hand all the time. I had to have a good supply of nappies, mashed-food and so many other things to make sure his needs could be met. When we left the house, we didn't know how long we would be away, or even if we would be able to return. Our cars were packed to overflowing, and I still had that feeling there was more I would need.

One thing I did well was keeping River's routine, it stayed the same as much as I could make it happen. I think that really helped him to get through the trauma without too much effect.

Because we had been around a lot of family over Christmas, it seemed normal to him to be around lots of people. I think he thrived on having all the activity around him, but I was always conscious of giving him a quiet space to get his regular naps.

When I think of the preparations, I did handle the packing and getting valuables pretty well, but I wasn't ever really calm. I found those weeks pretty stressful. If I had to go through it all again, I would definitely do some things differently, like having a better fire plan.

I would also get Ben on board sooner to prep the house. We left that too late. Even though we knew what had to be done, not much of it actually got done until the day of our evacuation.

Ben and his Dad and Mace all had houses to prepare, so they were helping each other. They set up sprinklers and pumps and tarps—but we all knew that if the fire came through, the houses wouldn't survive. They're all wooden homes surrounded by bush. We're more conscious of what is laying around the property now. We want things as far away from the house as possible.

I'd also try not to stress so much, I held so much in and was tense the whole time. I should have talked about how I was feeling. I was able to debrief with friends, but not until a while after, because everyone was going through the same thing. Nevertheless, that support network—family and a group of mum-friends who kept in contact as much as we could—brought a lot of relief, breaking the sense of isolation and breaking down the fear factor, too.

Fear verses faith—that was pretty hard. Whenever I felt my fears rise up I tried to be practical. I would get organised and I would pray. When we left here in a rush to head to the evac centre, I was just trusting God that whatever was going to happen was in his hands. Even when things got worse, I just knew it was going to be fine, that's when my faith really helped.

If I have any advice for other mums, it is to keep routine as normal as possible. I tried to stay as calm as possible so River didn't feed off my stress, but I don't think I achieved it very well. It was just too out-there, too unbelievable and unpredictable.

Looking back, I'm grateful for a number of things. I'm grateful that I took the time to get River's favourite things, that even in my rush and stress, I made sure I took them. I'm grateful we could all be together and we felt reasonably safe most of the time. And I'm really grateful that we had a home to return to; that it has rained and the fires are out and we can all breathe again.

Games children play

The children often proved just how resilient they were—and how observant they had been. My grandkids created a game that went something like this: One of the kids would pretend to have a phone up to their ear, 'Ring, ring, hello, could you deliver ice to my address please?'

Willow, obviously the ice company delivery van: 'Yeah sure mate, what's your address? I'll get my esky through soon.'

This pattern was repeated over and over until all the kids had 'phoned' through and Willow had delivered ice to them.

Obviously without power, there were no fridges, so the kids had picked up on how ice was a precious commodity. Without prompting from any adults, they were just playing this game as if it was the most natural game in the world. It did our hearts good to watch them deal with their stress in creative ways like this together.

We also encouraged our kids to eat lots of nutritious foods because this supports a stressed-out body and mind. They live like this normally—with my hubby being a nutritionist, our kids and their children are all pretty switched-on to these things. Fortunately, there was lots of clean, pure water donated from Coles, so we kept that up to them. None of them are used to sugary soft drinks anyway. While the kids ate mostly healthy meals and snacks, we made sure they were allowed the occasional indulgence because even not-so-good foods can be 'good for the soul' when used sensibly and sparingly. It also added a bit of a party atmosphere for them, to have the treats. We tried to make it seem like a great big family holiday as much as we could.

Physical touch is another important consideration that helps to reset the body after stress and trauma. Plenty of hugs and kisses and words of endearment went a long way to restoring our grandies' sense of security and of being safe. Having said that, we needed to be sensitive to the different ways different people interpret and receive love. Some of them thrive on physical touch, whereas others needed more 'space' to properly recover. Living together during this time we really noticed this. The kids didn't have their own rooms and all their familiar things around them so it was difficult for them when they needed alone time. Some would withdraw to one of the bedrooms for some quiet time, while others would snuggle up onto your lap whenever you sat down. Others of our kids just loved playing games together, sharing a jigsaw puzzle, or reading books.

And of course, our community is right onto the needs of our children. All the teachers were prepped before school went back and free counselling was made available for adults and children. Professionals who are trained and equipped to deal with this type of thing are a godsend. The important thing is that it requires work and effort by both parties. Counselling is a two-way-street in that it requires the kids to enter into the process for it to be successful, as well as the parents staying informed as to what approaches may work best for each one.

Triggers of trauma

There are so many triggers, not just for the children, but for all of us. Just the other day, a group of women were sitting chatting and we heard sirens. The wind was up, fire danger was at a 'very high' but things seem semi-stable because of all the rain we've had. Yet, our conversation stopped and someone breathed one word, 'fires'. It is an automatic reaction to what we have been through. Who knows whether the siren was an RFS vehicle or ambulance or police? Our minds have been temporarily programmed to 'fire'. We're all working through it.

It didn't help that on January 23, 2020 fires flared out of control, yet again. And yet again, my daughter Kelita was caught in it. They say 'lightning doesn't strike twice', but this fire doesn't care how many times it strikes. In Narooma, where Kelita was working, the sky went dark, the wind whipped up and the town transformed into an instant ghost-town within minutes. For two hours my daughter sat alone in the office, wondering what to do, no customers coming or going; the shops around her shutting their doors and putting the all-too-familiar 'closed' signs up.

'Her breathing became erratic as memories of what she had been through became real. It was a terrible ordeal to go through again—triggering many emotions that hadn't previously fully surfaced.'

Kelita messaged her family and we all begged her to come home. She was 72 kilometres away from her family—an hour's drive away on a good day. 'Please take it easy,' we pleaded, but come back to your kids. Shut the shop. And come home.'

None of us knew the fires had flared between her and us. We knew the potential was there for it to happen, and reports were warning it was going to happen 'later', but Kelita was to drive right into it!

Our poor daughter. She put the phone on speaker so we could talk through some of the worst of it. I attempted to coach her through, but the flames, the red sky, the darkness, the smoke-covered streets, the unknown, the uncertainty, caused 'flashbacks'. Her breathing became erratic as memories of what she had been through became real. It was a terrible ordeal to go through again—triggering many emotions that hadn't previously fully surfaced. She was desperate to get to her children and to all be safe. She didn't know how big or widespread the fires were, but she drove on and got through another 'end of the world' experience where nothing was as it should be, and nothing seemed able to survive the absolute chaos and danger and threat completely surrounding her.

Careful what they hear

Returning to our children, and from the days in the evac centre and beyond, we also tried to be conscious of what we allowed 'little ears' to hear. This was no easy task with so many different people milling around, talking fires continuously; some dooms-day prophets all too vocal about declaring the end of the world or making ridiculous statements like, 'the whole of the Bay will go up'. Kids never need to hear this kind of talk and we do all we can to protect our kin from it. Sometimes we would let our guard down and be discussing topics that children aren't mature enough to handle or process, but whenever we noticed one of the children in the room, we'd put that conversation on hold. It was more productive to use our family times, especially around meals, to discuss positive and reassuring things together.

Though we attempted to put these practices in place, it's no guarantee everyone walked away without some sort of effect. Everyone, every person we know, has been affected by these fires. It has been horrific. It is the stuff that nightmares are made of and so we need to make room for one another, not take offense easily. Being kind and patient, because grief can be a strange thing, and does not necessarily follow a predictable course or time line.

I'm no expert on this stuff, I'm just gleaning from my six-decades of life and I can see that grief and trauma are upsetting us all differently, which is why I'm attempting to allow for different expressions of it in each of my family, and why I'll never give up on a person, young or old, when they don't respond when I'd hoped they would. Everyone needs time to process this trauma; time to figure our own personal journey forward. For the grandies, this could take a while, for others of them, like my eldest granddaughter, they may feel they have already dealt with it. All responses are okay, there's no right or wrong.

Interestingly, during the second week of February, Kelita and her hubby attended a seminar on helping deal with kids in trauma, just one of the great resources our town is providing. Kelita said it was informative to know the tools she has available to apply to her own situation.

Kelita

The biggest challenge for us at the moment is consistency. Our kids crave it, we're craving it, but how do we achieve it in the whirlwind that seems to be our life right now. With everything so up-in-the-air, we really need structure. We need to know how the day looks, how the weeks looks, even how the month looks.

We're finding little pockets of it. I think the clarity for us comes in realising there are things that bring us so much joy and then trying to eliminate those things that don't bring us joy at all. Like allowing the kids to just play, not thinking about anything else.

Yesterday I took the kids to the beach. I had to screen out the fact that the water looked putrid and the beach was littered with thick ash and seaweed after the rains have emptied all the dirty creeks into the ocean. Once I did that, I just joined the kids, playing in the waves and laughing. I laughed and I felt it in my body. I can't remember the last time I felt that.

Place of prayer

For Step and I, as parents and grandparents, our biggest weapon against this trauma having long-term affects upon our precious grandies, is to pray. They're all used to it, we're a Christian family—so we pray with them and over them regularly and often. During the fires, it was continuous. We didn't need to be asked; everyone needed prayer. We endlessly found ways to instil hope in the children.

This empowers them as they learn to lean on God, knowing that they're never alone. 'You might lose everything, but you can't lose Jesus,' as Cassia has been teaching them. It also serves to help them feel more in control. Where there's hope, we can all look forward. We can all believe for things to get better, and begin to recognise the signs of things getting better. For example, by showing the children the new shoots beginning to sprout on the trees that were burnt in the fires, or letting them feel the wet grass under their feet after the rain, helps them to be reassured the fire situation is no longer a threat.

After years of doing this, we know only too well, how powerful and effective prayer is and how many times it has saved the day for us. When any of us are troubled, for any reason, we pray God's grace and goodness over them, and his peace to rest upon them. And I couldn't recommend it highly enough.

'After years of doing this, we know only too well, how powerful and effective prayer is and how many times it has saved the day for us.'

'We had so many new emotions that they were hard for the kids to talk about. They couldn't name them. The younger kids especially can't express it all—the emotions and the fears.'

CHAPTER 9
Needing company

I want to continue unpacking the experience of children through this bushfire disaster and help us to hear their voices. Across the community, our children are the unnoticed reservoirs of so much emotion and even trauma. I believe we all need to take time to listen so we can support each other in supporting them.

When things settled down, as February began and things got into some sort of 'normal' routine with school and packed lunches and time with friends, I sat with some of my grandchildren.

With varying responses to the trauma they had suffered, a few agreed that during the fires they got to the point where they couldn't sleep. Looking back, they don't think they were scared of the fires; it was more about needing company and not wanting to be alone during all the times when they were unsure about whether their families were evacuating or not.

The older kids agreed that they're not completely comfortable with change. Some of them enjoy being organised and the blackouts put them out of routine. 'Without lights on, everything changes, you can't do what you normally do. I like everything to just stay the same,' one explained.

What seemed to surprise them the most during the whole time the fires were threatening their friends and family, is that the fire got to them. 'Honestly, I didn't think it would!' another agreed. They'd heard so much about them but it was kind of 'pretend' or something until it got here and it was threatening their homes and neighbourhood.

On the day the fire came within 100 metres of our eldest granddaughters' home, they were fairly prepared, having packed suitcases and bags. One packed most of her clothes and a tub of shoes. Because their photos were on devices, they packed these and hard-drives, feeling organised. They nodded together that their Mum was on top of things way in advance, just in case the fire ever got near their home.

To the children, it initially seemed like there was plenty of time to get things together and get them to the cars. But casual packing turned frantic when some of them were unable to breathe. With face washers over their mouths and noses, they threw in a book or two, devices, everyday stuff, all the while attempting to be calm, now admitting they experienced some fear when they were separated from the rest of the extended family. The children all wanted to be together, but fires had blocked the roads so some had to head south, away from everyone else.

When the colour of the sky was mentioned, such as when the whole sky was yellow and an eerie orange, they nodded among themselves that they might have been scared then too, especially because the whole of that day the Mums were telling the kids all the fire updates whenever they had reception.

Interestingly, it was unanimous in what had made them all feel better—being able to gather with cousins and their Granny and Pa. Having the extended family together played a major role in the way the grandies were able to deal with the fires and process the trauma later, agreeing that it got their minds off the fires.

Thinking about having to evacuate, most of them took everything they considered special, and in the end, this process helped them clean-out their rooms. The girls agreed there was 'heaps of stuff' which they realised they didn't really want.

Those grandies, who were able to go back to their homes between evacuations, said they were most affected after the fires by not being able to access normal things, like groceries

'Another reason for the push toward minimalistic living is the fact that almost all of us know someone who completely lost everything, so drawers and cupboards were being scrutinised for things we could give away.'

or going out to dinner and celebrating school holidays, because their parents were out of work 'and so we didn't have much money'.

While at the Coachhouse, I was impressed with my eldest granddaughter's level-headedness throughout the ordeal. During our time together, she was a huge help with all the little ones; nothing was too much for her. I guess it was as good a therapy for her as it was for the rest of us, to concentrate on the wee ones and keep them occupied and happy.

My older granddaughters made some good observations, as there are many people who are experiencing the same thing about the 'clean out'. They've returned to what we can almost call 'normal' life and realised how much within their homes they had been prepared to live without if it came to that, so it has kind of sparked a time of 'minimalising'. Another reason for the push toward minimalistic living is the fact that almost all of us know someone who completely lost everything, so drawers and cupboards were being scrutinised for things we could give away—possessions that would bless someone else, someone who had nothing.

There isn't anybody who hasn't been affected in some way, and as more and more stories emerge each day, people are noticing little differences within and around them—and caring, giving, generous hearts is just one of the gems the fires have left us.

My youngest daughter's eldest daughter, Willow, 10, is another one who likes order and structure and for everything to stay the same. Unfortunately, nothing stayed the same for her for a very long period of time. Her and her family's lives were heavily disrupted.

Jordan

Mace, the five kids and I were evacuated a number of times, to three different places through November, December and into January. In-between evacuations, we were often 'on watch'. It was a time where none of us could really relax. Everything was on high alert and high adrenaline!

I think the first time we were evacuated in November, we panicked. It was a new experience and we really didn't know how to handle it. We were in shock. When the school closed on those intense heat and 'high alert' days, it just threw everything out.

The first time we had to prepare to go, I just stood in my kitchen in a bit of a daze. I mean, what do you take? How do you look at everything you own, everything you've worked for and collected and things the kids have made over the years and have to choose what is worth keeping and, well, what isn't? Basically, you have to ask yourself, 'what could we live without?'

I started with our paperwork, all the important documents and birth certificates and I took photos of everything. I grabbed washing baskets and Mum and I went through each of my children's rooms—taking what we thought they would want to keep. We filled their pillowcases with favourite books, their pyjamas, fluffy toys they like to sleep with, things like that, and wrapped it all in their doonas so they'd have their own bedding, wherever we ended up.

Some of the things we grabbed seemed least important— like fluffy toys and their favourite books—but they turned out to be the most important. It brought familiarity, comfort and routine into the chaos of some of the situations in which we found ourselves. Oaky, our four-year-old was saying, 'All my special things are with me, all the stuff I love.' You need to hear that from your kids.

It was hard for us, because we have five kids and we have worked really hard to start to get some nice things, so we wanted to take the new bedroom suite and the new lounges we had saved for. We finally had some nice pieces of furniture and didn't want to have to start again. A local firie came over to our house, through the long driveway cut through the bush and said, 'If you want to keep anything, get it out of here.' So that's what we did. We borrowed a small truck and started hauling everything we could out and into it. Even a pot plant that had taken me ages to grow, ha-ha.

It was a really weird season—we prepared to evacuate six times in the three months. We were evacuated three times. The first time, we went to Mace's Aunty's Surfside home they had just moved into. Their bedroom was upstairs, so we set up as best we could and all crashed downstairs, with most of our stuff kind of thrown into the garage. We evacuated back to their house a month later, but then they were given warning to evacuate from there, and the last time we were sent to the Coachhouse. At all the places we went, we still weren't sure if we were safe. We were told to evacuate from Mace's Aunty's the first time, but we stayed. It was too much for all the kids. Some of them were showing signs of anxiety. And we didn't even know then, that this was going to go on for months!

We learnt a few 'tricks' each time we prepared for evacuation. We started to notice what was important to our kids. Trying to keep some routine for them was really important. They needed stories at bedtime. When they woke up in the mornings they had their showers and got dressed, even if school or work had been cancelled. We wanted them to go through the 'normal' everyday routines so there was some stability for them.

We all slept together in one place. We didn't separate or have any of the kids feel alone or abandoned. We always prayed their familiar prayer at bedtime. And we gave extra cuddles. I took my time to do their hair each morning, just so that there was a bit more physical touch.

We had to talk about emotions without making it too obvious we were talking about emotions, if you know what I mean. We had so many new emotions that they were hard for the kids to talk about. They couldn't name them. The younger kids especially can't express it all—the emotions and the fears. They would best express themselves through drawings, their prayers, stories and 'pretend books' where we'd use our hands to make up stories and pretend we were reading a book.

For Willow my eldest, it wasn't so much about the house burning, it was fear of the unknown and where we would go. Our prayers became focussed on our safety; asking for God's protection and provision for us, no matter what. We would thank him for our safety and that we were all together. Things that she could see and feel. We watched our wording of prayers so that the kids didn't ever think that God ignored us.

When his cousin's house burnt down, it was hard for Hayz, our six-year-old son. He and Harper are really close. Hayz was really upset. 'I don't want Harper's house to be burnt down,' he would say. He needed distractions so he didn't keep thinking and worrying about it. He needed 'normality'. We evacuated with his whole book series he loves, all 10 books.

He had to be proactive—giving things to people, like his little red motorbike he gave to Granny to give to H the very next day. He needed to see his Daddy, his Uncle Benny and his grandfathers working to protect our house.

We also evacuated with Hayz's 'Mario Player' Nintendo Switch and games that he loves playing for downtime so he felt like we were at home. Something he could 'escape' into away from the stress of the adult world around him.

As Music Directors, our Church became a very big part of our recovery plan throughout the whole time. Not only for faith and family, but it served as a great distraction, having to organise music practices and night services on top of the Sunday morning service. Having this 'stable' regular routine helped us all. As a family, and as individuals.

What would I do differently? I don't think I would stress as much or rush so much unless we were 100 per cent certain the threat was real. There were a lot of rumours about where the fires were and when they were about to 'hit'. I would have liked to have been a bit more on top of that. Also, I'd be ready. Don't unpack yet... or yet...

To help her children through all the uncertainty, Jordan wrote this beautiful and insightful piece, through the eyes of how she thought her eldest might be processing things. It is added here with both their permission.

'One day I hope we can just live like we used to...'

It was a week before my 10th birthday the next time we got evacuated. I was sure this was it. I remember thinking, 'At least I'll get some new things for my birthday, and then I can start again.' But I really didn't want to have nowhere to invite my friends for my party.

My parents were acting weirder this time. I don't know if they were scared, but they seemed really worried. They even had some loud 'conversations' (fights) in front of us and they never do that. I was already so scared, I just needed to know we were safe and together. When they told me they were just stressed and tired I felt okay, but I still didn't want them to be stressed. I was stressed. I thought, 'Can't you be okay so that I can be okay?'

When I heard my Granny say my cousin's house had burnt down, I really didn't know what to do. I wanted to cry, I wanted to see my Aunty and my cousins and cuddle them all, I wanted to see their house all burnt so I could believe it, I wanted to go home and get some special things for them to keep, I wanted to run away and hide under my blankets and pretend none of this was happening... but instead I looked at my Mum with a face that said, 'I told you so!' I was sad. I was angry. She had told me we'd all be okay and our house would be okay, but how did she know? It happened to them and with the wind that day, I thought we were next.

It took me a long time to calm down that night and I couldn't remember the last time I fell asleep without thinking about the fires. I asked Mum to stay awake and check the app all night in case we had to evacuate from the place we were at too, or in case our house was gone. I don't know if I was really worried about our house burning. I was more just scared that we wouldn't know the fire was coming and we would be trapped in it. Thinking about it makes my hands all shaky. But after my Aunty's house burnt, I felt like I just had more things to worry about. I held onto my teddy and prayed and prayed that the day would just be over and I finally fell asleep.

Waking up asking your Mum and Dad if your house is still there is really weird, but I think I kind of got used to it. It was every day for a few months. I don't know if they always knew, but they always calmed me down and told me all that matters is that we were safe and that a house is just a house. Sometimes I even got excited about starting again if we had to. But I'm really glad we haven't had to.

When I think about it now, I feel so weird. My body feels all hot and my hands get sweaty. I don't know what to call all of my feelings because some I had never felt before the fires started. It's been really tricky to talk to Mum and Dad about it when sometimes I don't even know how to explain how I feel. Even when I pray to God, I don't know what to say. Mum just prays for protection over me and I like the way that makes me feel. I'm trying to pray like that too and hoping God hears my heart.

We had to evacuate three different times with all of our special things, with lots of other days just watching and waiting. But now I think it's almost over. I'm still a bit scared to unpack everything. Sometimes I still find special things and put them in a bag just in case. One day I hope we can just live like we used to... comfy and happy to be home.

CHAPTER 10
Fear in the flames

At the start of *When The Smoke Clears*, I recounted my first-person experience of the chaos and emotion we experienced in the terrible days at the end of 2019. For the next two chapters, Kelita tells this story from her family's perspective. In her own words, she describes what it was like to be trapped in the fire, having to watch their home burn down, and the long path to recovery that continues. I hope every person who is a direct victim of the fires, such as losing their home, or worse, gets the opportunity to tell their story, to be heard. This is Kelita's story.

Kelita

The moment when I first started to think seriously about the fires was while visiting my friend Haley in Termeil and I saw where fire had surrounded her parents' home. It was to be another couple of weeks before it was to come to our house.

We'd been breathing smoke and having no real sunlight pretty much since September, so we were very aware of the fires (who wasn't!), but I guess what we weren't aware of, was how close they were. Nor had we ever faced a threat like this before. I was worried about other friends when the fires burned Bawley Point early in December, but never really had any fear of anything coming our way. Because the fires were on the news constantly, heaps of friends were regularly messaging to see if we were okay; I always shrugged it off, like, 'Yeah, we're fine. It's not in Batemans Bay.'

Sometimes my husband would say, 'If the fire gets to Catalina, we're screwed.' But I'd reassure him, 'We're fine. It's not gonna get to us, we're in a built-up area.'

'We all knew the fire was out there somewhere because the smoke never went away, but I always thought we'd be okay.'

Then just before Christmas, Long Beach was evacuated and we took a family of evacuees into our home with us. Our house was their safe space. While they were here, I was seeing their stress and could sense their fear but didn't think fire would get to Long Beach. I still kept thinking, 'It's fine, it'll all be okay.' Never once did I feel stressed or concerned about it coming into Batemans Bay.

After a great Christmas Day with extended family, on Boxing Day, my little family went camping in our caravan out to Congo (near Moruya). Some people had warned us not to go, but even when we were there, I was thinking, 'We're fine, we won't need to be evacuated.' When we were told to go, I still thought we were being evacuated as a precautionary measure and never once did I think about fire reaching Catalina where our home was. I think I'd become desensitised to it. I just wanted everyone to stop stressing and being anxious all the time. I wanted to enjoy the days we had holidaying with the family and forget the fire. We all knew the fire was out there somewhere because the smoke never went away, but I always thought we'd be okay. The furthest thing from my mind was that it would hit Catalina.

There were so many previous evacuations that had amounted to nothing. Everyone was so over-prepared to start with and then when it happened on New Year's Eve, it caught us all by surprise and nobody seemed prepared.

On December 30 we were advised to evacuate Congo the following morning, early. Our friends didn't want to have to leave at 4am, so they packed up their tent and we sent them to our house to stay overnight before they travelled back to Canberra. We thought our house was the safest place in the world.

New Year's Eve arrived and everyone at the campsite was up early preparing to leave. One minute we were fine and then it was a mad panic as word got through, 'Quick get out of there, Congo is going!'

Congo never 'went'. But if it did 'go' that day, we would have been stuck right in the middle of it.

An automatic text came from the RFS at 9.30am telling Batehaven and Surf Beach residents to 'evacuate as the fire approaches your area'. And then we got the official text about evacuating Catalina. My hubby said, 'Noooo, that's not good,'… and everything just went crazy from there. We sent my husband's brother, who was staying in Hanging Rock nearby, to go to our house and check on it for us while we attempted to get out of Congo. While he was there, he phoned to say that there were spot fires in our neighbour's yard and he was putting them out. He said, 'It's very hot and very smoky here. I've watered everything down that I can. The planes are flying over with red retardant. It's so hot, I can't stay, I'm getting out of here.' The service was really bad. The towers were down and he was cutting in and out. There were only tiny bits of service so messages were coming through from the RFS for people to evacuate, when the fire was already there.

The RFS just didn't have the manpower for how big it was. As well, there were so many powerlines and trees down that some roads were closed and firies couldn't get through.

Trying to get home

By then, we were in our cars, not sure if we could make it through Moruya to head toward home. We had heard that the bridge was going to close and they were evacuating the town. So I went across the bridge first. You couldn't see what was in front of you because of all the fire and smoke. When I got to the other side of the bridge, I phoned my hubby to let him know that he could get through with the caravan and that his Dad, who was behind him in his car, towing his camper trailer, could make it too.

From then on, we travelled in convoy, my hubby leading, me in the middle with the three kids in my car, and his Dad behind me. We had to go along the coast road, as the Princes Highway had already been closed. Everything was a mad panic. As we travelled toward Tomakin, the sky was a deep red like the whole world was on fire and it was thick with smoke. Nobody was safe to drive in these conditions. We were so disheartened because we knew there was no way we could get through and we just wanted to get home to our house.

As we pulled into Tomakin at 9.51am, the fire-brigade and police put barricades over the road; we were the last cars to get through. That left us trapped at Tomakin at 10am. We had to sit tight there until we heard otherwise. By 11am everything was completely black.

We had our three children with us and it was freaky. I kept thinking, 'They are going through so much'. While stuck at Tomakin, I could see fear in Harper's eyes. I looked around and there was panic on everyone else's faces. Spot fires were flaring up on the grass in front of us and someone had been injured and was on the ground being treated by a nurse while they waited for an ambulance to get through. We couldn't breathe outside, so we jumped into our caravan, thinking this might calm the kids. We felt trapped inside the van, the smoke was so thick and so hot outside that we had to close all the windows. We were in there sweltering, sweat pouring off us.

H kept saying, 'I don't want our house to burn down. Please pray, Mum, please pray.' It was so intense that it felt like nobody could survive. 'I don't want to die,' H said again, 'Pray, Mum!' He was lying on the bed in the van, while I was trying to feed my youngest, all curled up with his eyes tight shut and his hands together, freaking out. I prayed with him about 14 times. Here's where faith hits the road. It was that whole dilemma of how does our faith help us overcome our fear. As long as H was asking me to, we prayed. We needed a miracle and we believed for that miracle. We prayed for our safety, and in the middle of our fear, believed God would get us through this. We were running out of oxygen inside the van, we couldn't breathe, but outside was red hot.

We were there for three long hours, hardly able to breathe, my kids freaking out, none of us knowing whether we were going to get through this. The fire felt on top of us. I've never felt heat like it. I don't even know how to describe it. Like an open furnace or raging bonfire had gone out of control—or like we were thrown into it. The effect of the heat was as if you'd been gut-punched, it sucked the breath right out of you. We were intensely hot—so hot that we were dazed, even our brains felt fried so we found it hard to think. It couldn't have been hotter or scarier. Also, it was difficult to console my children when I had no idea of what was going to happen, myself.

Our street is on fire

Then we got word that, 'Catalina and your whole street is up in flames'. From a vantage point some distance away, looking up toward our house, my brother-in-law had seen a house on fire near our street and could see that the trees along the middle of our street were up in flames.

My hubby kept shaking his head, saying, 'Our house is not gonna survive.' I tried to stay optimistic and I was saying, 'Yes it will. They're obviously onto it. It's gonna be alright.'

Later, we were to discover that planes had dropped retardant in the area, but it missed our house completely.

After hours in the stinking heat, sweating like mad, we were fearing the worst but just had to get out of the caravan—we were suffocating. The sky was pitch black. There had been sirens and helicopters going all day. Everything around us was crazy. We saw someone's front yard catch alight in front of us.

'My husband received a call then and after his father talked with him, he sped off. Then his father came to me and said, "Don't rush back, your house is gone."'

Incredulously, at 12.42pm, the southerly hit—and it turned freezing cold! It brought with it a sense of relief that it was over. The cold wind on our sweaty skin felt like ice. It was freezing. But it wasn't over. We had been lulled into a false sense of security.

We didn't want to stay at Tomakin. We knew the wind had changed so we were free to try to make it to our house. We couldn't believe what we were seeing! All around us, as we drove through Rosedale, homes and bush were on fire and then through Malua Bay, again, everything was on fire. There were fires burning on both sides of the road and we saw houses burning down.

We could hardly breathe in the car so I got the kids to put their clothes over their mouths and noses as we drove. I was glad to be in the middle of the convoy, my little car hemmed in between the two big rigs. We all stopped in Malua Bay because it was difficult to see very far ahead of us, and we thought we were stuck, again. It was difficult to make any sense of the mayhem. My husband received a call then and after his father talked with him, he sped off. Then his father came to me and said, 'Don't rush back, your house is gone.'

His father had advised my hubby, 'Don't drive like an idiot. Your house is gone, there's nothing you can do.' I was in shock. I just sat there stunned. The kids were in the back and there was commotion all around but all I could do was sit there. My house was *gone*? It didn't even compute. We eventually made our way through the fires, past burning houses like it was a warzone. The other two cars drove straight to Hanging Rock where my brother-in-law was staying.

I drove, with the kids, to the house.

I drove past fire trucks at a house near my street and when I got to my street I saw that there were houses that looked okay. So, I had this fleeting hope again, that they were wrong. That our house was still there and it would all be fine. Then I saw there were powerlines down across the road in our street and I couldn't drive any further. I looked ahead through the smoke and flames burning in the trees all around and could see that the tall tree from the next-door neighbour's yard had fallen and crashed over my driveway, so there was no way I could get to my house anyway.

I could see my house. My children could see. The structure was still there. But there were flames leaping out of it everywhere. It was 1.30pm. As soon as I saw that, I thought, 'Okay, my house is burning down.'

It wasn't safe to stay where we were. All the tall trees were on fire and any could fall at any moment. I couldn't keep driving around my street to get out, so I had to reverse down the one-way street, in shock, thinking, 'My house is burning down.' I drove to the in-laws at Hanging Rock, and by the time I got there my husband and his father had already left to see our house. He arrived there at 1.42pm.

I didn't see my husband. Instead, everyone who had evacuated to my in-laws' house was coming out and giving me and the kids hugs. About 20 minutes later, my hubby came back and then we just fell into each other's arms and had a cuddle and a cry. We continued feeling numb throughout the rest of the day.

Our phones had some reception, so we were trying to get a hold of other family and friends to tell them our news and to see how they were. We were both just in shock. Our kids were running around in the backyard... playing.

At 7pm we braced ourselves and together, we went back to look at our house. There were little spot fires still burning inside, glowing in the darkness. The fence had fallen down and the house-number was on the ground. We picked up our number nine and took a selfie.

That metal number off the letterbox was all that was left of our house.

That night was probably the hardest night of our lives. There were so many moments where my husband just lost it and broke down. We were devastated. We were exhausted mentally, physically and emotionally. After camping for a week with all the kids crammed into our caravan, the thing we were looking forward to the most, was getting home to our own beds. Saying prayers and kissing our kids goodnight in their own rooms. And that can't happen… ever again.

CHAPTER 11
Where to now?

Kelita

We were staying with the Hanging Rock family for a couple of nights and then it got a bit hectic with all the people that had been evacuated there, so we decided to get some space and moved to the holiday house next door. After just one night, we were moved on, as other families were also being evacuated to this house. Friends had offered their grandparents' home to us. This brought a little hope as we grabbed the keys and moved our few belongings in. As soon as we looked around, we realised it wouldn't be practical to live there. It was a pristine home with beautiful furnishings, not kid friendly at all, so just wasn't suitable for us.

We were feeling defeated.

For the next few weeks, our phones didn't stop beeping with texts and phone calls, everyone sending condolences. We had 80 to 100 messages a day and I wanted to answer each one personally, because people were showing so much love and kindness. But it was exhausting. People began offering us things we needed, but we had the dilemma of nowhere to put anything. We just ran on adrenaline that first week.

Then came the Coachhouse. Though we could barely hold our heads up by then, it was such a relief to have, not just somewhere to go, but somewhere where the kids would be safe and with their cousins. We were all together. It was so healing.

Though it was small and cramped, we felt so grateful. The unit had no bed for Lennox, our one-year-old, so he slept with us in the double bed.

'People began offering us things we needed, but we had the dilemma of nowhere to put anything. We just ran on adrenaline that first week.'

We had no routine, everything was so unsettled. The kids were up late every night and they all wanted to sleep with us. Oh, the lack of sleep! Our minds were so active! My skin went crazy with the stress; breaking out in itchy rash on my face. The kids' skin broke out and they were covered in mosquito bites. Lennox couldn't stop pooing. His bowels still aren't right.

Yet there were many highlights for our family at the Coachhouse. We had a roof over our heads and we were safe. It was the first time we had our own space; knowing we had it for as long as we needed and wouldn't be moved on in a few days. We could relax. Being together with my family was nice. We had huge family support and the kids were happy when they were with their cousins. Not that it felt like we were on a holiday, but we kinda were.

We were to enjoy the hospitality and love of Kellie, Gonz and their beautiful daughters and all the team at the Coachhouse for 10 wonderful days.

The kindness of strangers and friends

And then, on January 13, 2020, after a really 'natural' meet-and-greet and working things out with the owner, we were given a private rental holiday home on Denhams Beach, provided through emptyhouses.org for the NSW South Coast—where over 100 empty houses were listed and 89 families registered their need for a home. They worked to match as many as they could and their page now reads, 'It has been so rewarding to witness the difference that the generosity of strangers can make for those who have lost their homes.'

Definitely a breath of fresh air and answer to prayer, for us. We couldn't believe Lawrie and his family had donated their beautiful home for people like us. We can't thank him enough. It is difficult to put into words what this act of kindness means to our family. When you have nothing and someone offers what seems like 'everything' there are no words for it.

Lawrie didn't want anything in return for giving us his home, all he asked was that we covered our bills. We'd been pretty disillusioned before that, being offered places that didn't suit at prices we couldn't pay. But Lawrie and his family went above and beyond to accommodate our family. They put themselves out—*that's* kindness!

We all connected straight away. He loved us and we loved him. We all just clicked and since meeting and agreeing on the terms in a semi-legal fashion, the arrangement has grown into a friendship. He genuinely cares about our family. We just think he is one of the most beautiful people on the planet. With Lawrie coming into our lives, it has shown us the love of God 'with skin on'.

When we first moved in, it felt so good to be able to spread out. We felt free for the first time since the fires. We went down to the beach in the afternoons as a whole family and tried to restore some sense of order. We did all we could to get the kids' rooms set up for them. And we tried to get them ready to go back to school.

All during this time, as word got out to more people that we were homeless, more and more possessions were being offered. It was a time of lots of heartache and pain, balanced by incredible loads of kindness and love. The donations kept coming, we had offers of everything from cars to toys, clothes and furniture.

There was a lot of good amongst our heartache. People are very thoughtful and generous; the gifts came in abundance and we are so appreciative of what people have done for us. I think all the kindnesses will become more real when we have our own home one day, and we can look back and remember all the people who believed in us when we couldn't see our way forward and we'll be forever grateful.

We were given so many clothes, and at first, we just wore what had been given, whether it suited us or was our size, or not. It didn't seem to matter as there was still no hot water for anyone to have a shower and no room for me to get 'made up' and we had no energy for anything. And it was so hot because the fires were still around, so we didn't need many clothes anyway. The kids just needed something cool to throw on. So, it didn't matter. But eventually, we could be pickier, as more donations came in, because we had so much offered to us.

Out of this situation—that I wouldn't wish on anybody—another good thing has been reconnecting with old friends. It makes you realise what's important in life and how everything is so... unpredictable.

You hear those sayings, 'you never think it'll happen to you' or 'here today, gone tomorrow' or 'life is short'. And then you get it. They make sense.

I had a couple of amazing friends, Sarah Borrowman and Lauren Barlow, friends since we were 18-year-olds, ask our permission for a 'gofundme' page. They called and said that they wanted to set it up. At first I thanked them, but said no. Cameron, a friend of my husband had already offered to set one up and we'd told him that we didn't need help. Then, after a day to think about it, we agreed that it probably wouldn't hurt.

So, I phoned the next day and said to the girls, 'If you're happy to go ahead with it, that would come in handy.' We were thinking we'd be stoked if we received around $5,000—that would be a real blessing—and it reached that tally on the first day! And then it just kept going up and up. Within a few weeks it peaked at $25,865. This unbelievable gift from so many people was miraculous to us. People from all over the world were donating. It was truly humbling and such a relief all at the same time. The money helped immensely with immediate needs like our rates and phones bills. It continued to help because my hubby lost all his tools in the fire and is without work. We have used it for general living expenses and what's left will help toward a deposit for a new house… when we get to that. For those who gave, we really want to thank you. You wouldn't believe how much this means to us. Until you're in a situation like this, where all you have is the clothes on your back (and all we had were our ratty old camping clothes), you don't know what every small act of kindness means.

I am so humbled and inspired by all the people who are making a difference in our lives. They have given time and money to us, have shown interest in our family and our needs. They have been giving what they can and have lifted our spirits so much. It is difficult to describe what it feels like to be the recipients of so much generosity from strangers and friends. We have been treated with compassion and with love. The kindness of so many overwhelms us at times and we just hold each other and thank God.

We've been in the Denhams Beach house for a month now. We're so grateful to have somewhere to lay our heads and be able to retreat to from the chores we face each day. Though it seems every day rolls into one, the support has been amazing. Strangers rallying together for us. Even people I hardly know have been doing whatever they can for me. So many people offered to help us out. There's a real sense of community; everyone helping each other. Not just here in Batemans Bay on the South Coast, but from all over Australia and to the other side of the world.

So many have lost their homes here and Australians have delved into that community spirit for which we're known around the world. They've banded together to raise us up. It has brought out the best in so many people. I love watching what is happening. Nothing given is in vain. Any clothing I've received that doesn't fit me, I've been able to pass on to the other girls I know who have lost their homes. Everyone is giving, there's no appeal that we don't give to. We're a 'look out for your mates' kind of culture, and I love that about Aussies.

Dad's cousin Allison Tarrant and her husband Wayne brought a whole car load of goodies from their friends and neighbours in Campbelltown. They brought them to the Olive Tree and all of the nine families within our church that have lost their homes or been severely impacted by the fires could rummage through and get whatever we wanted. There were high shoes that fit me perfectly and some really nice outfits I could wear for work. The kids got clothes and toys. It feels so nice to have people doing these things for us.

Despite all this love being poured out on us, the reality is that we still struggle with feeling low. We're tired and drained on a daily basis. It is like we are waiting for things to go back to normal, but at the same time we know it won't.

Faith through it all

I'm so glad I've had my faith through all of this. No matter what we've been through, never once have I thought God failed me. I do think there has to be a reason behind it. Once you understand that God gave us the earth, and bad things can happen to anyone, you don't cast blame anywhere.

And I know He can make the bad, good. I believe this. As much as our situation sucks at times, I know that through the bad, God will bring good. Don't get me wrong, I've definitely had 'down in the dumps' days where all I want to do is cry, but I feel that is all part of the process. It is what it is. God's in control of things and He loves me and my family.

I feel His presence the most when I'm driving to work, listening to Christian motivational talks. The general message is that, 'If God brings you to it, He'll bring you through it'. And then He makes the impossible, possible. And no matter what we're going through, I know He'll get us through it. Life is designed in such a way that we're meant to be doing the hard bits with God. I do often think whatever I'm going through, He's with me.

Imagine if I didn't have God! I wouldn't know what to do. But I can give it all to Him. I've never felt alone. The more life goes on, I realise I have to endure suffering. In the end, it's good for the soul and it gives me empathy toward others who are going through their own struggles.

God has been a source of comfort. I'm thinking now though, I used to pray with the kids, a general prayer at bedtime. I haven't done that recently and want to get back into that routine. The kids need it. We sing a worship song every night when they're going to bed. It's a little ritual that brings them calm. Something that can stay the same when everything else around them is different.

There's a lot of things I want to start doing, like being more focused about routine. When you go through a crisis like this, everything goes out the window. Yet routine is the best thing; it's probably what we're lacking most right now. We also have new routines, with London going to preschool. We have a lot to get sorted.

Hubby is off work; I'm working a bit more so we have a little bit of money coming in, which makes me more exhausted. We don't want to use all the fundraised money at once; we need that for a deposit to start again. Someday soon, we hope.

Don't ask me about this last month. It's a blur. We really didn't have a summer holiday. Everything was messy and smoky and then destroyed. In the last month, my kids have started back at school and hubby and I have needed to go into the recovery centre, with our baby in arms, every day. Every single day. We've tried to get our documents back; we're going through the process of grants and government funding. I feel like there hasn't been a day where I've had nothing to do—and I really crave that.

But amongst it all there is much to be thankful for—we're living in a house where we have ocean views; living in paradise, surrounded by family that support us, and a huge amount of love from friends near and far. One highlight is that me and my hubby have grown closer and stronger and have been able to spend more time together.

And we look forward to the fact that we will get a new house, eventually, and we do get to start a new chapter. This is just the 'in-between'.

CHAPTER 12
Dare we unpack?

Let's pick up the story from where I left off in Chapter 7. We had survived another horror week of fires and evacuation, celebrated Ben's birthday on January 11, and greeted the second Sunday of the year with a prayer of gratitude. Now, what's next?

Ah! The absolute joy of *stopping!* In the whirlwind that has been our life on the South Coast all year, there was nothing better than to pause for a moment, take a breath and wiggle in some room to breathe, so that is exactly what happened for me the very next day, Monday, January 13. I hadn't realised how tired I was. I hadn't realised how much I needed to just stop, have a home day... my first relaxing home day at the Love Shack since we had officially moved in.

Little did I know how valuable and essential my simple little chai ritual would prove until crisis hit and 'routine' and 'sameness' quickly became worth far more than gold. I mixed my spices, heated my almond milk and stirred it all into a nice bubbling broth, which I transferred from stovetop to teapot. I got out my 1970s cup and saucer and watched the steaming brew flow into the cup. I placed it all beside my open Bible, grabbed a pen and my favourite notebook and lay on the carpet on my tummy. This little regular ritual took me to a place of peace, a time of calm stillness. The true value of having daily calming rituals shone through that morning where I didn't have to go anywhere, be anywhere or flee anything.

There's an audible sigh of relief this Monday morning as I felt game enough and safe enough to unpack our precious belongings from Buzz. Though word has come that next week we'll see danger levels rise again, I was keen to put those thoughts waaay back in my mind and 'play house'. I hadn't had somewhere to call our own for nigh-on 10 years, so I was keen to set up my nest after a life of travel in our van Buzz, even despite the nagging feeling that it may all need to be packed up again within a week.

Step and I had planned to be helping at a working bee at one of our friend's properties, but it was cancelled at the last minute, so the thought of having the entire day to unload and unpack seemed a rare luxury. Clothes, food, important documents, family photos and other random paraphernalia that seemed crucial to save at the time, came out of Buzz and into a home covered in a thin layer of ash and soot; reeking of smoke.

Desperate for normal

I'd been buzzing around all the previous week helping others, so was glad of this time to just chill—though it be cleaning and unpacking—yeah, that's how desperate we were for something 'normal'.

There were some, those who seemed semi-sorted, who made themselves available to assist others who were not so fortunate. Some were beginning major clean-up jobs where walls, bedding and furniture all needed work to remove much thicker layers of debris and smoke damage, while other possessions needed replacing. Nobody knew what to expect until we all started heading home to see what state our homes were in. And yet there are still others, though ever so grateful for their small space in the evac centres, who are desperate to find somewhere to call 'home', be it temporary for now. I have a little weep as I think of them and pray for them. I can't imagine being completely homeless. I can't imagine building something up over a lifetime to have it all wiped out in one day. There are many who will be fighting for resources and manpower to rebuild and reshape their futures.

'Some are feeling guilty for laughing or moving on with their lives during this tragedy, but shining our unique light is even more important for healing, wholeness and recovery at this time.'

After a few tears, overcome by even trying to envisage what others are going through, I savour another cup of chai to sip. I feel the tension release in my neck and shoulders; tension I hadn't realised I was carrying. It's the simple little things, cuppa time, recharging my body from somewhere deep in my brain's memory that tells me all is okay. And it is okay. We have God; we hold His hand as He has our backs. It has been Him whispering sweet love songs above the roar of the past chaos and the chores facing us. And we have each other—Step and I, our family, our precious community, our tribe, our team—where hugs speak louder than words and love helps heal wounds.

We are rebuilding. We have brooms and mops in our hands.

Later in the day I find myself reassuring someone that it's okay to have fun. Some are feeling guilty for laughing or moving on with their lives during this tragedy, but shining our unique light is even more important for healing, wholeness and recovery at this time. There's a Scripture that says, 'The joy of the Lord is our strength,' and oh boy, do we need strength!

On Tuesday, January 14, the day after my day of rest when Step and I cleaned the Love Shack and all the grounds, I had organised to meet some friends for breakfast—Kim, Angela and Kathie. We were happy to simply spend time being in the moment together before I head out on my next delivery run in the Buzz-mobile. We cried, shared stories, hugged and laughed together, but mostly we made sure we had some healthy strategies in place for self-care and positive mental health.

In our giving and grieving and going, it is important to sit, stop, strategise and share.

When we take care of ourselves, we're energised and equipped to help take care of others. We felt good healing together, because, it is together that we win.

Kelita had been in contact to let me know that St Anthony's Primary School were arriving with three vehicles and trailers to deliver the precious donations of backpacks and school supplies to the South Coast. Harper and London posed with their new bags after going through all the new bits and pieces. Kelita shared their story with the team and allowed them to see firsthand the excitement and happiness their donations give to those they reach. It seems we are in two states constantly these days—the horror of what we've been through, and the gratitude for those helping us rise up out of it. London and H wore their backpacks all day, only removing them now and again to make sure all their new stationery supplies were still in there, safe.

Capturing joy

I seem to have my phone out all the time, snapping pictures whenever I see joy. I capture a picture of my youngest grandies all gathered within the arms of their older cousins enjoying being encompassed within a safe space. Through some of the symptoms of trauma and grief they are occasionally displaying, it is good to record that they're loved, snuggled, adored, doted-over, (sometimes fought over) and reassured. Watching this love in action always reminds me of a trustworthy saying, 'God loved the world so much that he gave...'

That famous John 3:16 quote is seen in action throughout our community at present. Loving arms, hugging others, comradeship and reassurance, offers of help and lots and lots of unconditional giving.

And that's when we all got together again for a different kind of 'Last Supper'. We shared a very special night, all of us evacuees, as we said our farewells and thanks to Kellie and Gonz and their girls, along with their staff, for an extraordinary couple of weeks. It is incredible the bond we have been able to form during this wild and crazy, unforgettable time as grateful evacuees and volunteers. The media were there; doing a special shoot of this special place. Camera operators, after clicking our photos, shared the meal with us.

It wasn't the first time media people, for one show or another, had joined us... Kelita had already appeared on worldwide news after being interviewed by the Al Jazeera network news crew. (Later, in early February, Kelita and her family were filmed in their temporary home for NSW and Australian networks.)

Though we tried to articulate just what their sacrificial, over-and-above care and love meant to us, there really weren't enough words to describe Kellie, Gonz, their girls and the crew at the Coachhouse. Lauren covered it beautifully:

Kellie has gone above and beyond for her community over the past few weeks, doing more than I can say or probably will ever know. Firstly, helping tourists evacuate and providing them with what information she had in order to get them home safely. Then her girls stepped up, helping do head-counts and record information of who was still in the park, no small task, delivering messages, bringing in supplies, entertaining the little kids and the list goes on.

Then she opened the park as an evacuation centre, providing meals, housing and emotional support to hundreds of people. It was Kellie who organised food and supply deliveries so no one would go without. She knew who was in the park by name and listened to each of our stories. Kellie and Gonz frequently passed on information and set up a fire plan to keep everyone safe. All this while still keeping a calm atmosphere. She is stronger than I think she knows and has put so many before herself and her own welfare.

Your family and community are very blessed to have you Kellie Whittington. We hope you get some rest soon.

Then on Wednesday, January 19, with the Relief Centre set up and manned by Army Reservists, locals like Kellie had an opportunity to stop. Wow, we had to take our hats off to the Army guys, serving us with strong arms carrying supplies to our cars and their big hearts making us feel welcomed and important. From heatwave to downpours, they offered smiles and assistance. Working out nappy sizes for my grandson proved Wednesday's funniest challenge, but the gentleman on the personal-hygiene stall who could advise on the benefit of pads with 'wings' got my biggest salute!

It didn't matter who I dealt with at the Relief Centre after that, I was always treated like royalty! An Army Reservist from Sydney bent over backwards to help Mia and I gather free groceries and water. He joyfully carried it to Buzz, called us by name, popped his hat on my granddaughter's head for a photo with her and beamed proudly to be serving his country during this crisis. And he invited us back to do it again. What a lovely experience to uplift our spirits. They have been just one of so many teams doing Australia proud during this difficult time for our communities.

A level-headed hero

One such kind-hearted, level-headed hero is Batemans Bay RFS Captain Ian Aitken. As early as November 21, just days before the devastating Currowan Fire began its unstoppable rampage towards the coastal oasis of Batemans Bay, Ian had an uneasy feeling about this fire season which had started unusually early with fierce fires breaking out across Northern NSW. After fighting Grafton fires at the beginning of November, where he found himself in the hairiest situation of his career and actually fearing for his life at once stage, little did Ian know he would return home to face a fire front just as ferocious.

While fires were hundreds of kilometres away from Batemans Bay, Ian had predicted that the exceptionally dry conditions, high temperatures and strong winds would precipitate a similar fire event to the one experienced in 1994. Twenty-five years ago, fire had burned a path of destruction through numerous Batemans Bay suburbs, but fortunately only one home was destroyed in that blaze. Ian's concern was that should bushfires threaten the area again and follow the same historical pathway, hundreds of homes would potentially be at risk.

At 2am on New Year's Eve, Ian's worst fears were realised as he saw the Araluen Road Fire advancing down towards Mt Wandera. He saw it creep slowly down from the north west and into the gully at the base of Mt Wandera. Once it was on its uphill path, it had gained speed and was shooting flames high into the air. Later that morning the two major fires that had been threatening the Eurobodalla dealt out catastrophic consequences! By 6am Mogo was blasted with a fire storm that nothing could have stopped. Conditions were so extreme and so volatile that people were being advised to 'get the hell out of the way of the fire' and basically leave it alone to do its malevolent work.

On the very same day, fires to the north and to the south, ripped through West Conjola and Cobargo, causing horrendous damage and loss of life.

Ian, his wife Connie (who was hands-on through the entire ordeal) and I caught up over cuppas and homemade cookies while they took me through some of the whirlwind that was the life of volunteer firefighters and their families through December and January.

RFS Captain Ian Aitken

After Mogo, the fires blazed south and east, taking out hundreds of homes in Jeremadra, Malua Bay, Rosedale, Surf Beach, and eventually Catalina. Because everything erupted earlier than expected on New Year's Eve no one was prepared for the assault.

'...with embers and burning debris hitting our windscreens all the way through. I kept thinking, "This will only be for a short while", but we drove for kilometres through a burning inferno.'

With only a handful of local crews available, and with Strike Teams from Victoria either heading home or replacements still on their way to the Bay, there was nothing we could do.

On New Year's Eve after being out on the fire line all night, we had to drive through the fire, burning on both sides of the highway, dodging flames from the left and then the right, with embers and burning debris hitting our windscreens all the way through. I kept thinking, 'This will only be for a short while', but we drove for kilometres through a burning inferno. My crew were trying to get people off properties to safety, but some chose to stay and defend. Nobody realised the ferocity of what was coming at them. In the end we were telling them exactly what was coming—we wanted them to realise how serious the situation was and then we had to go and warn others.

After working all night fighting fires, I headed home in the morning to sleep. I turned the radio off and tried to rest but I couldn't get the fires out of my mind. I just had to get up and I went straight back to the fire front. I answered a call to the industrial area, officially putting myself back on duty. We responded to a call from Bay Auto and saw Beta Electrical go up. It was all hands on deck by then. Everyone turned up. We thought we were ready for it, but this caught everyone by surprise. It was a freak thing. The fire we faced came through hard and fast and with great ferocity. It was a volatile raging monster! I remember someone saying, 'Armageddon is on its way.'

I have to say that I'm so proud of our team. Everyone did

so well. Our station turned into a staging area where we ran operations. We fed the volunteers, organised the lunch and dinner packs, sorted logistics and worked with local businesses. Then the power went out.

Coles was fantastic—they opened up and allowed us to take what we needed. We were cooking barbecues for 200 people from the RFS, Strike Teams, National Parks, Forestry and others.

We had generators to keep the station running while all other local stations were without power. The partners of our firefighters turned up and pitched in. It was back to basics, we just kept working—laptops on every bench. We didn't know what was happening in the outside world, we just kept going around the clock. We had team members crashed out on stretchers in the station so they could be around to take emergency calls.

As Acting Divisional Commander leading the brigade and staging area, I couldn't be prouder of the way everyone got stuck in. It was organised chaos, where everyone had a job to do. And although we were all tired and fatigued from constantly fighting fires, living on the edge and sleeping with one eye open, everyone was serving and helping and working together.

The next few days were absolute chaos with power and communications out and hundreds of homes and outbuildings nothing but smouldering piles of rubble. Even after such a severe battering by the fires, there was no end in sight and definitely no time to relax. The weather forecast for the coming Saturday, only four days away, was catastrophic! Fortunately for us, the conditions weren't as extreme as those predicted and we made it through the day with only a few spot fires and minor fronts to contend with. We were still reluctant to back-burn in places because the conditions made all fires unpredictable and incredibly risky.

From November 26, 2019 to February 16, 2020 we were busy—very busy. The fires continued to threaten the region until the end of the period, when the NSW Rural Fire Service announced that, 'For the first time this season so far, all bush and grass fires in NSW are contained'.

Assessing the aftermath

It was only after the smoke cleared and we could do a thorough assessment of the damage, that we discovered the extent of loss. 501 homes had been destroyed, with an additional 274 homes damaged. There were also some 600 outbuildings and sheds destroyed, and an unprecedented 79 per cent of the entire landmass of the Eurobodalla burnt. Apart from the surpassing tragedy of losing lives in the bushfires, Batemans Bay and the Eurobodalla Shire was the worst affected region this year, across the nation.

You may ask why I do it. Well some people play golf, others surf—I fight fires. I started 20 years ago in Moruya and came back to the RFS in 2003. I think volunteering is in my blood. My Mum volunteered through the Uniting Church and Dad was into scouting. I grew up watching my parents volunteer in their community. It is like giving back or paying it forward.

Now, for us here, we will conduct a very thorough debrief— we've earned that. We were able to protect properties and save lives in horrendous situations. Considering what happened, the warning system worked extremely well, without it we would be seeing a lot more funerals.

We'd like to see a prescription plan, a systematic way of reducing fire fuel and getting hazard reduction in place, talking with the Indigenous and some of the older people of the land. It is important for people to understand that fire seasons are getting longer, so a possible recurrence could happen a lot quicker than last time. I had been saying, 'This time bomb is ticking,' for a month before the fires broke, and I'd predicted it would follow the same path as the 1994 fire. We've had our lesson from nature. Now that we have gone through this, we are moving forward so that we can be better prepared for the future.

Everyone needs to have a fire plan. Everyone should be fire wise and fire aware.

As for our team's personal welfare, we have the Critical Incident Support Service in place. Under normal circumstances, if I notice my people having a hard time, I get CISS to give them a call. But with what we have been through, I gave them a list of the whole team. CISS will look after them and give them the on-going care they need.

Now we are working on our after-action review (AAR), where we keep the discussion positive and open and allow everyone to have input. We discuss what we were intending to do and what actually happened. We look at what worked and what we need to do differently. Reviews are a healthy exercise because they help with training, they keep people prepared and they indicate what strategies are needed for the future.

I'm full of praise for the volunteers and their families, everyone really did pull together with such courage and determination even though the odds were stacked against us. There are so many to thank—my crew and the community for their help during such challenging times and the many businesses who came on board when we needed them most.

With all the donations, RFS has the funds needed to upgrade all of its facilities and equipment. I know some of the things I'd like to see in place, including an audit on all stations so we can upgrade our sheds and equipment to be better prepared in the future.

I'm in the process of training to be Group Officer overseeing eight brigades. It's a very busy job, everything will end up in my lap, but that's my goal for next month. What's keeping meetings lively now is the influx of volunteers joining the RFS, which is a great outcome from this appalling time.

While people are taking notice, now is the time to get a fire plan in place. 'Hazard reduction' by Forestry, National Parks, Councils and private landholders is only one part of the picture, with many other things needed. I would advise that everyone has a fire plan, it's what has saved lives here and will in the future.

Ongoing trauma

Because things just don't 'heal' overnight, even with all the assistance we are getting, many people I'm talking to feel they are just not getting a break. There is so much destruction all around us—and every conversation seems to be about the fire.

On January 17, I had a children's writing workshop scheduled and some of the mothers had asked if I intended to cancel the event. At first I thought that would be the easiest thing to do, but I began to get a sense of how much it was needed.

After icebreakers and some funny writing, we got down to the nitty-gritty and of course, the main topic was the fires. Two of the children attending had lost their homes and most of the others had been evacuated, some a number of times, or experienced loss of sheds and other buildings on their properties. It was a raw and real workshop, where I allowed the children to express themselves any way they felt comfortable. Among the rainbow unicorns that could pooh out smarties, were stories of pain, blood and killing things. This isn't unusual under trauma. Kids need to lash out somewhere—it might as well be in a writing workshop where their words could release a lot of pent up confusion and fear.

I felt honoured to be able to conduct the workshop and have the children respond so openly and freely. Of course, we also had word games and too many lollies—but it showed me the need for 'natural' therapies where big issues can be dealt with through drawing, writing and play. We all left pleasantly exhausted.

Not surprisingly, many people throughout the community were showing signs of trauma as January drew towards its end. Friends and family members were beginning to show signs of stress and fatigue, anger and exhaustion, confusion or impatience—it looked different throughout each phase of the journey, but all of it was trauma-related. By now, members of the community were being diagnosed with Post-Traumatic Stress Disorder (PTSD) and seemed to be walking around in a daze of pain. With destruction so visible and tangible, our trees still down and the roadside chaos reminding us of what we've been through, it was a stark reality check for me that life may not necessarily get back to 'normal' for some time. My daughter's block hadn't been assessed or cleared, they didn't have any housing, my son-in-luv was still out of work, school hadn't gone back, friends were starting to break down during conversation and there was an overall feeling of exhaustion over us almost as thick as the smoke had been. It was definitely a very strange time.

The news reports no longer featured us, so it was beginning to feel like the rest of the world had moved on, and we were left here, broken and damaged, with nobody strong enough to pick up the pieces. Everything had changed. Our environment had been raped and pillaged by the fires and many were finding their mental state just as violated.

Jordan

I had a few of my kids in the car, on the way to visit a friend who lived on the other side of town. Instead of being able to take the usual roads—it was still like a battlefield with roads closed due to damage from the fires—I was sent on a detour. I didn't worry too much about it, because I know the area well. I've been living in this region for 10 years. Strangely though, I ended up feeling lost and it kind of scared me.

There were trees down along both sides of the roads, everything familiar was burned and many of the road signs were either burned or removed—about to be replaced. The tall trees I must have subconsciously used as landmarks were black and lifeless to the point where I couldn't recognise anything around me, until I felt disoriented and ended up getting lost in the places that I used to know. After a few more turns, I felt like I was on a completely different journey. I got to my friends' place, but had an unsettled feeling to shake off so I could clear my head and have a conversation. It is very disconcerting to get lost within your own familiar townships.

I, Chrissy, spent the morning of Tuesday, January 21 enjoying breakfast in Mogo and morning tea in Batemans Bay. Actually, this was the beginning of how I intended to spend my mornings in the future, supporting local businesses.

The day was bright, but there was destruction all around. I was seated comfortably in a safe space but it hadn't been a safe space here just weeks ago, that's for sure. Half of Mogo was gone. Destroyed. It was my first time travelling down into the once quaint village that used to be surrounded by thick bush, tall trees and had been renowned for its carefree lifestyle. It was heartbreaking to experience it in such a ruined state. I felt traumatised at first, seeing shops I had loved, completely gone; seeing the old church burned to the ground; seeing the bush for kilometre after kilometres just brown and black and uninhabitable. It was a difficult trip and even more difficult to sit still at the café.

Still, I enjoyed a lovely interlude at Grumpy and Sweethearts with my good mate Julie (more details to follow). After she left to tend to her errands, I had a wander around. I wanted to purchase some things, do some shopping to lift the spirit of the place. I purchased some items for the Love Shack, coloured rugs and cushions—and was surprised by the welcome I received—hugs, thanks and such gratitude toward me simply for spending some dollars. It showed how raw the wounds were—at that time Mogo hadn't received any of the fame that has been lavished upon it since. Mogo was still our sleepy little village where the shops woke at 10 and went to bed at four during the week.

One of the shopkeepers discounted my mats because we had been fire-affected and another salesperson helped me carry cushions out to Buzz, hugging me and holding me tight in gratefulness for my support. I had tears trickling down my cheeks as I drove north back toward Batemans Bay. There aren't many incidences where I'm not moved by the beautiful community spirit that has risen from the ruins.

Eyes on the good

As I drove back through the black, bleak bush that used to be thick and teaming with life, I realised how important it will be to keep my eyes on what is good. Not just my physical eyes, but my 'heart' eyes. I need to see it, feel it and appreciate it. I have to find the good, and when I find it, I need to share it for the benefit of someone else who might not quite have found it yet. That's the way I see it. We all need one another. Community is such a powerful force. Funny how shopping can have that butterfly effect.

A café a day

My beautiful Lauren had tagged me in a *Café a Day* campaign. I do like to be out and sharing a cuppa with someone nice and early. It still leaves all day to get things done, but begins the day well. It can be a juggling act for me because I like to swim each morning. I also like to bushwalk, but it's been way too hot to go for my regular walks. I'm not sure how I got out of the habit of this so quickly, considering I've been a walker most of my life. I guess a disaster can do that—throw everything out the window until you don't even know yourself.

I'm a regular morning walker and have been for years and years yet I haven't been out walking in ages. Not only could there be snakes about, but there has been the persistent threat of fire. And still, there's something else niggling at the back of my mind. I think it is the fact that none of us want to be too far from home for too long. It is still early days. We're weaning back into life and we're giving ourselves time to allow that to happen. There's no rushing through this process—healing can be a gradual thing.

And it has made me realise that I want all my loved ones around me. I'm back into smother-mother mode, I think; texting them each morning to see if they want to have a cuppa with me, making sure they touch base so I know they're alright, wanting to connect just for the reassurance that we're all still here.

I can't demand too much from my family though, so I gather with girlfriends. Some days I line them up, back to back chats so I can get to more cafes. Grumpy and Sweethearts in Mogo (as mentioned), followed by Starfish Deli and then the Innes Boatshed in the Bay's CBD, beside the Clyde.

Tribe Café, my second home, snuggled in front of Birdland where the deer call to one another and crazy peacock sounds fill the air, is where I'll spend tomorrow morning. Birdland was scorched by fire, but managed to survive, similar to Mogo Wildlife Park; both remained closed to the public for a time while damage was assessed and animals calmed.

I love the funky vibe at Tribe Café—and they certainly make the best chai. It's an eclectic setting and the chai tea is served on a board, with the teapot and honey all set out in the ritualistic way that I love. I can guarantee that if you come to Batemans Bay and order a Chrissy Chai at Tribe, they'll know exactly what you're after. I can continue my morning ritual here and that's important to me right now.

There still aren't many people about. I understand that it could be due to the strange, slow healing process underway within hearts and homes. What I do know is that within every café, I have been hugged, fire stories have been shared and everyone is glad to be alive. Despite the loss of property and homes and vehicles, we're still here!

There has been so much loss for everyone to deal with. Fires are still burning, but we are no longer on high alert or under threat. We want to breathe a sigh of relief, but most of us aren't quite there yet. Many of my friends don't want to jump the gun, they're content to slowly emerge. I can appreciate that.

At Mossy Café, where my eldest granddaughter works, cheeky Rainbow Lorikeets don't mind nibbling your toast straight from your plate. At Grumpy and Sweethearts, bold lizards come up to my toes, scampering over my feet while the not-so-bold, tiny finches are flitting in the garden bushes beside me.

As mentioned earlier in the chapter, I spent a lovely morning with Julie there. It was time for us to catch up again as I hadn't really seen her since her house burnt down in the New Year's Eve fires. Amazingly, she had already been able to find a light at the end of the tunnel and even back then, was excited to share what her future looked like despite her loss. There were glimmers of gold within the rubble and she was remembering furnishings and wall hangings she'd used for the sale of her mother's home in Bowral, which meant some of her treasures still remained. Julie was determined to purchase that house that you read about earlier—it actually happened! Of all the terrible things we'd faced, that was a nice thought to take away with us.

Grabbing help with both hands

The rest of January rolled on with a granddaughter's birthday celebrations, writing this book and two children's books with other grandkids, and helping Kelita, with the past few months of drought, fire and smoke taking their toll. Our days jump from cold to heatwave. It's been wild. As February begins and people go back to work and kiddies are back to school, we all feel like we're crawling out of a boxing ring. What we do now, I think, is crucial. We have to grab any help offered with both hands.

I want to continue to find ways to help others because it's my best self-help tool. I want to join with others helping to get our community back on its feet.

Thinking about January, that year-long-month of fire and smoke, I'm trying to move on with positivity. I need that positive energy to propel me into February and beyond because although we're still struggling, and will be for some time, it's also true to say our month was filled and overflowing with love in action.

For me, January rightly claims the title Love Month because never before in our history had our community pulled so closely together; never before had so many new connections and friendships been formed; never before had we experienced such abundant generosity beyond our imaginings; never before had so many put aside petty prejudices and joined together as one; never before had so many services been available to assist us mentally, financially and materially; never before had people shared hugs and tears with such openness; never before had so much of God's love been shown so freely.

CHAPTER 13

Rising again

One of our most memorable moments from the fire season—and there were many—was the video call we got through to our friend James, just as the fire front had passed his house on New Year's Eve. Now it's time hear this story from his first-hand perspective.

James

I can't even count how many friends have lost their homes. One of my mates had been in the same house for 35 years, with two of his sons living on his property and other than some of his sheds, everything is gone. He and I were at my place together and one of my neighbours who lost his home came over and joined us. It wasn't a planned thing but as we chatted over beers, we bonded. Then another neighbour who had also lost his house came over and I guess we talked together for about two hours. I call it burning bonding.

We all lost tools and other stuff that were meaningful to us, but we just had to let it all go. I suppose it's bonding and healing being able to talk, but it wasn't easy. After the fire went through, I was angry at what it had taken from me. The fire had changed my life in an instant. It had taken away my whole perspective; taken away my 'toys' that I'd worked hard to get. That feeling lingered for quite a while after the fires.

Before it happened, my girlfriend and I were at Runnyford enjoying time together camping. We had all worked really hard, helping the owner to clear the site so that we could be safe if a fire did come through. At the time there were rumblings

'After the fire went through, I was angry at what it had taken from me. The fire had changed my life in an instant.'

of how serious the fire risk was, but we were there to enjoy ourselves no matter what. The night before the fire struck, we were paddling on the river in a kayak and on a stand up paddleboard. Looking back, it was just so calm and beautiful and so it's hard to comprehend the difference to what came next. We were awoken at 2am with news that the fire was on its way to where we were camped. My girlfriend had received word from the RFS that the fire was really close.

We took an hour to pack up our tent and other gear and we headed for Batemans Bay lookout to see what we could see. From there we couldn't see much and so we headed home to my place at Malua Bay for a much-needed sleep. At 6am we were woken with the news that the fire was on its way to my place. With all our camping gear still in the back of the car I drove my girlfriend back to her home at Broulee. I was so conflicted—I wanted to be there for her and her kids but I also wanted to get back and try to save my home at Malua Bay. It was so frustrating working out what to do, we were both agitated and upset and my girlfriend had gone into quiet mode. Everyone handles stress and pressure differently and it was then that I decided I had better head back home and try to defend my property.

Face to face with the fire front

I seemed to have a lot of time on my hands and I didn't really know where to start. I spent the next hour moving things between my house and my shed. I kept thinking that steel can't burn so it seemed a safe bet for my surfboard, my ride-on mower, and my work tools to all go into the shed. Then I spent a good 15 minutes driving my car back and forwards trying to find the ideal spot before the fire front hit. I had an ample tank of water for fighting the fire but my hose only reached so far and I wanted my car close to the house so I could protect both.

I had a fire plan and had spent the past couple of months prepping for the fire, but I started to wonder whether the gutters needed cleaning again and whether I could have done more. I mixed up a sports drink, put on my ski goggles, my boots and all cotton clothes, but had to make-do with a wet tea-towel wrapped around my face. I was prepared, but at the same time totally unprepared for what was to come.

When the fire finally did come it burned slowly and gently, not like I expected. I had two big gum trees close to my house, so I thought it best to light the debris under them before the fire reached there—to reduce the available fuel. I reckon that helped a lot, that is until the wind hit and started to drive the fire front towards me. I waited for 45 minutes to an hour for the front to hit, and when it did all hell broke loose.

I was so scared and frightened by the heat and the noise, like a roar! Everything went really orange—a horrible orange! And really hot. I stood in front of my car hosing it and the house and then I felt myself go all wobbly and light-headed, my knees buckled and I nearly passed out. If I had, I would have been dead for sure! In one whoosh, the fire sucked all the oxygen out of the air in front of it, as the wall of fire came at me fast. My palm trees just exploded! Other things were also exploding around me and I was scared that I would die right there! After the initial fire front roared through, it left all my sheds burning while more fire just crept up through the bushes and slowly spread around me.

As the front went over me, I recall thinking, 'I don't want to be here'.

I got into my car to get out of the heat and to be able to breathe. I took some photos from inside the car and I could breathe for a moment, so I stayed until I was sure the front had passed. I felt safe in the car, I could look out and see what was

'Everywhere was black and burnt, with trees on fire all around us and the grass still burning. I saw the homes of neighbours who had evacuated, burning. I turned around and walked back to my house.'

going on. For about 10 minutes I wasn't sure whether I would live or die, I was really scared, but I knew there was no way out and that I couldn't leave in the middle of the fire. Once you've made your plan to stay and defend, it's sink or swim. There was nowhere to go, everything was burning.

After the fire front finally passed, I got out of my car. I started to hose everything down within reach and it was then that I received a video call, of all things, from Step and Chrissy. They had been concerned for me and I was so pumped-up on adrenaline I can't recall anything I said, but I think I jumped around and yelled about beating the fire and saving my house.

After that I walked to my neighbours to check on how they were going. As I neared their property, I could see their place was already up in flames and beyond help. At that moment I felt the brutality of the fire, how it had kicked so many of our arses. I wandered down to the next neighbour along only to find their place was gone as well. Everywhere was black and burnt, with trees on fire all around us and the grass still burning. I saw the homes of neighbours who had evacuated, burning. I turned around and walked back to my house. As I approached, I was horrified to see that the roof was now smoking and obviously on fire. Nooooooo! I was expecting to come back to my house and it would be fine. An ember must have caught in the gutter—it only takes the smallest amount to burn a whole house down.

For the next 15 minutes I went ballistic. I grabbed my mattock and a ladder and I climbed on the roof and started to hack away at it, but it was getting worse. I was so angry at the fire and how it wanted to take my house away from me. One of my neighbours was walking past so he rushed over and helped me. I had to get into where the fire was burning or else my house would go up just like all the others. I was running on adrenaline, going up and down the ladder and smashing the mattock again and again into the roof. After all I'd been through I wasn't going to give up without a damn good fight! I ripped up the roofing sheets only to find the insulation burning and the ceiling already black and discoloured.

I was so angry at that ember. How could it sneak up on me like that? It took ages but we finally got the fire under control, pouring water in through the hole. I had saved the house, but there was a fair amount of damage to deal with. The fire had burnt a decent section of the roof and through main stay beams, but there was also a lot of water everywhere inside, all through my loungeroom and my new couch.

Nowhere to go

I didn't know what to do, those of us who had stayed, were stuck there. There was no way out, so I walked up and down the street, I had to move. I couldn't believe how many of my neighbours' homes had been destroyed. I saw a neighbour's horse and it was pretty burnt. It was trying to move but its feet were too sore on the scorching ground. I wanted to get it out of the paddock and onto better ground, so went home and got some organic carrots. I couldn't lure it out though. It took me half an hour of trying to get it to safety, I wouldn't give up. I was running on adrenaline and couldn't fail at saving it. I tried everything, and in the end, I smacked its butt and it started to follow me.

It was now about 3pm and I gathered with a few neighbours as we began sharing our stories in shock. We were exhausted. One neighbour, he was just a legend. He saw two of his neighbours' houses on fire and fought to put them both out. That one guy saved three houses that day.

Trapped inside my head

I went back home, but looking at the damage did my head in. I was going crazy. My house was a mess—I was a mess. There was no communication; no anything! Without power, I had to light a candle. I tried to read a book so I didn't see its flame. I didn't want to look at any more fire. I drank some wine to counteract the adrenaline that was still surging through my body but my mind was stuck in overdrive. It was horrible. Everything was going on in my head and there was nobody to talk to. I was trapped inside my head. It wasn't until 2am that I finally managed to get to sleep.

The next morning I had to secure my roof because it was open and exposed and after all the water we'd poured into it, it had caved-in. I had to borrow a tarp from a mate to get the job done—I didn't even have a tarp, the fire had taken everything. I got wood to hold the roof up and spent all day trying to fix it. Inside was covered in ash, debris and gyprock, and water was everywhere—all over my new lounge, my big TV, and everything else in the room. I spent the next 3 hours mopping and picking up rubbish, but it was still a bloody mess. My girlfriend called and I told her I couldn't come over yet because I was mopping the floor!

Two days afterwards, I was still in shock. I went to the local IGA supermarket to get some supplies and because there was no power, internet or EFTPOS, the owner gave us anything we wanted and said we could come back later and fix him up. Everyone was just writing down what they took and he was giving credit until things were up and running again. I heard it was the same at the Batehaven IGA store as well. Their generosity really moved me.

It was dark and eerie in the shop without lights. There were only two other people in there, both from my area, whose homes had burnt down. One of them told how he barely made it out of the fires alive. He had decided to stay and defend, but the fire came through and burned his house down right in front of him. He was going to be trapped in there with the fire unless he took desperate measures. He bolted out through the bush, flames all around him, frantic to get to safety. Thank God he had a Holden! He only just escaped through the wall of fire, not knowing which direction to go or whether he would make it through. He's lucky to be alive, that's for sure!

Seven weeks on and I'm still waking at three in the morning with my heart beating wildly. The insurance company has assessed my home and a builder from Merrimbula has had a look at what needs to be done before I can live in it again. I've had three counselling sessions after the fire and I feel like it's been very helpful. At the moment I'm obsessed with covering as much of the destruction from the fire as I can. With free bark chips from the local tip, I load up my ute, then get home and shovel it all out again. I do this over and over in a manic state. I've been wearing myself out getting as many loads as I can because I'd rather look at the brown and red of the bark chips than the depressing black that's everywhere.

I also had a visit from Samaritan's Purse, which is a Christian organisation that focuses on helping out in areas that have been affected by trauma or natural disaster. It was an amazing experience to have all these people I don't know, come to my place and help me tidy the mess after the fire. I was so thankful and moved by their generosity that I broke down a couple of times through the day, but I'm sure they're used to it. We worked for five solid hours together then we shared lunch and I got to tell them my story; I owed them my story. They were really lovely people and they listened to what I had to say. We prayed together as well, which felt good. One was a chaplain and left me a booklet to read. When they left I felt happy, comfortable, and reassured that everything would be okay.

There's still a lot to do before I can move back home. I'm slowly but surely getting things tidied-up and in order. Some of the burnt-out stuff has been removed from my block, a car and trailer, but there's still a lot more to be removed before it feels like home again. The shed is on the list for the NSW Government to deal with. I still have no power and the roof is still waiting on repairs, but I'm hoping that all will be well soon enough. Like everyone else, I just have to be patient.

One of the biggest issues with the fires is that my safe place and security has been taken from me. Once its dark out there, it reminds me of the fire. Even a big southerly wind brings back that 'returning fear'. I'm still not sure how I will go sleeping in the old place once I can move back home.

CHAPTER 14
The carers' view

I usually start my days with, 'Whatever you're up to today, God, take me with you.' But during the fires, I noticed I was saying more, 'Wherever I'm going God, please come with me.' I approached those days differently. The second prayer has a suggestion of doubt. But the first prayer brings peace and comfort and excitement. It's only recently that I noticed the difference between how I prayed during the trauma of the fires and how I'm settling back into my usual way of talking with God.

Looking at all this, as I'm compiling this record of events and emotions, it is difficult to know how we'll handle the trauma. If nothing else, this experience is showing us just how unpredictable life can be. There are no guarantees. Years ago, I had a breakdown that knocked me down for almost a year. In recovery, I remember deciding to appreciate each day. If I couldn't appreciate the entire day, I would at least look for something I could be grateful for. I would believe for those 'kisses from heaven'. I learned to pray during tough times and the good times, because God is interested in my thoughts and choices, He wants to be a part of that process so He can bring out the best. He wants to journey through life with me, constantly and continuously, especially during the hard times.

As I draw this book of stories to a close, it's important to hear from those helping others in the journey of recovery. Verna, a counsellor and dear friend, shared some thoughts on trauma at church the other day. With her permission, I am sharing them here.

Verna

Communities on the South Coast, as well as elsewhere, have experienced an unprecedented event with the recent bushfires. Everyone has been affected in some way.

Last week I attended a training night focusing on trauma and how it impacts people. It was run by a member of the Billy Graham Rapid Response Team in conjunction with Samaritan's Purse. These Christian organisations are here to offer practical help for people who have been affected by the fires, including clearing building sites of debris so that reconstruction work can begin. Their generous and self-sacrificing efforts remind us that God is right here with us as we work to rebuild our lives and communities.

One of our first objectives was to understand what trauma is and how it impacts people. Trauma is often associated with a sudden, unexpected and challenging incident that causes significant distress. This can include loss of property, physical injury and incapacitation, or loss of life. Whether trauma affects us personally, or whether it impacts someone close to us—like a good friend or a family member—both can have devastating consequences. People are often overwhelmed by a traumatic event because they feel like control of their lives has been taken from them. Two of our fundamental needs as humans are security and certainty. When trauma strikes, it shakes these foundations—sometimes violently—which explains why we can be moved so deeply.

Not wanting to underestimate trauma or people's suffering, it might be helpful to remember that bad things and tough times invariably happen to all of us.

In comparison to the frightening uncertainty that often accompanies trauma, we have a constant 'someone' who never changes, someone who is the same, yesterday, today and forever. This someone is God, and He knows exactly what we are going through, and what we need to deal with the situation so that we can come out the other side in one piece.

This reminds me of a beautiful promise Jesus made to the people of His day who were struggling with life, just like we do at times. In Matthew 11: 28-30, He said that if we come to Him in our time of need, we will find rest for our weary souls, and we will learn how to 'carry our load' through life without taking on more than we should.

Southland Batemans Bay, Senior Leader Garren Walton

This has been a huge time for our church and our town. While we have all been challenged by the fires and the destruction they have caused, I am learning that there are always good things to come out of tragedy and loss.

After the main fire burnt hundreds of homes and properties on New Year's Eve 2019, Cassia and I knew that we needed to prioritise time with those who had been affected, so that they could tell their stories and feel that somebody understood what they had been through, and were still going through. Our focus was on listening to people, praying for them, and generally offering what comfort we could. We were also aware that people needed practical and financial assistance to get back on their feet.

It wasn't long before we were inundated with calls from churches all over the country, with many offering financial support for those in crisis. Because of their generosity, we were able to buy stoves, water tanks, generators, pumps, food items, petrol vouchers, and to replace tools and equipment that had been lost. We wanted to provide for people's immediate needs, but we also knew there would be many needs to consider over the months ahead. People who lived outside of the affected areas could easily forget about the disaster and move-on with their lives, but we knew we were in it for the long-haul because this is where we live.

You are not alone

One of my aims was to have people know that they were not alone in this, that they could reach out for help and it would be there. We have seen this happen time and again as people throughout the community are pulling together and working together to make sure everyone feels supported. About three weeks after the fires, various agencies set up the Crisis Relief Centre at the local Soldier's Club, while the Army Reserve came to help distribute the truck-loads of food and everyday items that, in typical Aussie style, had been donated as soon as the disaster hit the news. Because many people are in a state of shock after a traumatic event like this, we also tried to put people in touch with the right services so they could receive as much help as possible, as soon as possible.

It wasn't long before the disaster, and the pressure of a long and drawn-out fire season, were beginning to show in people's behaviour and in their mental state. I was taken aback by the number of people—even those not directly affected by the fires—who were struggling with their mental health. Stress, anxiety and symptoms of PTSD were rampant, and anyone with underlying mental health issues and addictions seemed to be extra prone to relapse. It made me realise how many people are living on the edge and struggling with their everyday lives. It has certainly created a need for more support from Cassia and myself as we care for our church family and others in the community, but that's what we do anyway, only now it has become more of a priority.

Guarding against burnout

Because Cassia and I were on-call 24/7 during the peak of the trauma, we needed to guard ourselves against burnout. While we are called to comfort people in their stress and grief, we aren't called to carry it for them. We are there to help where we can, but only God is able to carry the heavy loads that life dumps on all of us from time to time. Cassia and I are big on

'We are there to help where we can, but only God is able to carry the heavy loads that life dumps on all of us from time to time.'

sharing everything with each other—especially the worries and responsibilities that go with leading a vibrant church. We discuss everything together—all the time—because we know that two heads are always better than one, and that a problem shared is not going to overwhelm us. We've been leading Southland Church for more than a decade now and we have developed some good habits that will hopefully keep us going for many more years to come and see us through tough situations like these.

I'm a firm believer that the best way to be of use to others is to keep ourselves in good shape physically, mentally, and of course, spiritually. It's like a bank account—unless you make regular deposits, you can't expect to have cash available when you need to make a withdrawal.

In our position as leaders we are mindful of our need to take time out to relax and unwind and just be ourselves. We do this by planning regular dinner dates, going on bushwalks, and getting away for a night or two together, either by ourselves, or with our two girls. In times like these we all need, and often crave, a dose of 'normality', where we don't have to think or talk about the smoke and the fires, and don't have to look at the depressing scenes around about.

Even though the challenges have been extensive over the past couple of months, and especially so since New Year's Eve, I know that our church people have grown through this. It makes me proud to be part of a church that is so willing to include and embrace people from all walks of life, even those who don't share the same values and ideals as us. For years now we have been known as 'the church without walls'—not because we have only just moved into our new facility, the Olive Tree, toward the end of last year—but because our vision is to see the 'invisible walls' that, at times, separate the church and the community, come down and stay down.

Nobody likes the idea of suffering and hard times, least of all me, but when we look for the good and positive things that rise out of the ashes of disaster, we can be assured that we will recover from this. Hope is rising, and with God's help I know our community will be stronger and more resilient than ever!

CHAPTER 15

Hope grows

I'm remembering a rather stressful day at the evacuation centre as we watched flames leaping in the distance, yet even amidst the pain and turmoil and strange mood among the adults (or perhaps in spite of it), the children were outside dancing. God bless the little children. They can teach us so much. I love how they instinctively know the importance of releasing tension through play. It is a shame we lose this natural tendency as we 'mature' and we forget the simple pleasures of a life well-lived. Like dancing in the wind.

The wind was wild. The girls were using it to propel themselves into pirouettes and spins. Their hair flailing and their skirts spinning, they were having the time of their lives... while we were indoors. We watched through the windows while we were holed-up in the cabin, possibly stressing more than we should have.

Many discussions back then centred on what could happen and the *what ifs* of another unpredictable day ahead of us. We knew the winds were detrimental to fire containment. We had knowledge of the damage the wind could do in those extreme conditions.

And then there were the children, dancing. Just thinking about that moment captured in my memory at the Coachhouse Evacuation Centre reminds me that we will get through this. There is joy in the journey—even a tough unpredictable one!

I take a big breath. Inhale and exhale loudly. I can do that now. And it doesn't hurt my lungs. And I don't have a coughing fit afterwards. A Facebook post comes to mind. It is a SC Lourie

'I take a big breath. Inhale and exhale loudly. I can do that now. And it doesn't hurt my lungs. And I don't have a coughing fit afterwards.'

quote; 'Breathe, darlin', this is just a chapter. It's not your whole story.' Difficult to comprehend in circumstances that seemed all consuming. In the thick of it, there didn't seem a way for the 'story' to continue. We had stress pressing in on every side; our chests hurt from the smoke that filled our lungs and fires threatened to consume our peace and possessions.

Beauty was there too

And even as I reminisce over this past seven weeks—the wildest seven weeks of my life and certainly the most dramatic for my family as a whole—amidst the pain and the black and the broken and the damaged and the uncertainty, beauty was there too. It had to be. And we drank it in over board games by candlelight, or playing ball games with the kids, or catching soldier crabs on the mudflats while planes and helicopters scooped water out of the river, carrying it over our heads away to the fires. We found it and embraced it in the meals we shared crammed around a too-small table in a too-small cabin, while so grateful to be able to stay together. We found it as we served meals and washed dishes for the hundreds of others who were in the same predicament as we were. We discovered it in the kindness of a pat on the back or a smile coming from deep within an otherwise wounded soul. We enjoyed it in the bags of chips and bottles of water provided free for us to enjoy. We savoured it in the reading of stories to the children at bedtime. We appreciated it during our brief, cold showers and finding a clean pair of hippy pants to put on. We needed it. And beauty was there. That was the kind of faith that those days called for.

I'm reflecting on those harrowing days now. Here in the safe space of the Love Shack. God bless those amazing heroes who fought relentlessly. They never backed down. RFS, SES, police, ambulance, volunteer rescue workers—though the flames leapt high over their heads, their determination to quench them reached even higher. There were some incredible human hearts, true heroes, who fought valiantly to see this town saved. And largely, they did it. Hats off to them all. Their sacrificial efforts saved so many.

I was speaking with a firefighter's wife one morning at Tribe Café. Whilst sipping chai in the uncomfortable heat of another scorching day, she shared stories of her husband's bravery and the emotional and mental stress he was under during the long shifts. I know some firefighters who were feeling guilty about having four hours sleep before they headed back out to fight the dragon for 12 and 16 hours straight. They didn't want to stop. They didn't want to fail anyone. Visualising victory, they just wanted to keep fighting. Incredible what the human spirit can endure. Mighty men and women fighting in such extreme and dangerous conditions, to save the homes of people they didn't even know. To save our town. We are one. There are no strangers, we're all part of the whole and ever so grateful for it.

A time for thank you

None of us would be where we are today without some amazing humans risking their all for us. While it is true to say that hard times and tragedy bring out both the best and the worst in human nature, I want to take a moment to acknowledge the many unsung heroes who will probably never receive the credit they truly deserve for the sacrifices they have made. At the top of the list are the brave and big-hearted firefighters who have given more of themselves, and of their time, than most of us would do in a lifetime for others. The people of Australia— and particularly the people of the Eurobodalla Shire whom I represent here—thank you from the bottom of our hearts.

When we think about your courage and your bravery, in such extreme circumstances, we are in awe of your willingness to sacrifice both your time, and your safety, for us. Thank you for continuing the great Aussie tradition of self-sacrifice and mateship in these challenging times.

So many organisations jumped into the fray to assist. From free counselling sessions, legal assistance, insurance advice, housing and welfare, to recovery and dispute resolution services. Funding packages were made available for those seriously affected by fire including emergency grants through Red Cross up to $20,000, injury grants up to $7,500 and $5,000 grants for home repairs. The Salvation Army offered financial assistance, emotional wellbeing and support services along with referral and advice teams. There's up to 10 mental health treatment services through Medicare; advice on distress interventions, coping strategies, social supports and family-based psychological interventions. CommBank released up to $50,000 Bushfire Recovery Grants for community organisations and schools. Tradies For Fire Affected Communities had skilled tradesmen around the country putting their hands up to donate time and skills. Australian National University provided up to $2,000 with upfront expenses for laptops and study materials; the Indigenous Land and Sea Corporation established grants up to $20,000; Regional Tourism grants became available to support events, and festivals were offered in an attempt to lure visitors back to our region. The RSL provided for veterans impacted, the local Council offered a range of support, such as waiving development application fees and rates deferment. The Wildlife Heroes Program had funds for increasing the number of wildlife emergency responders and increasing the number of wildlife able to be rescued and cared for.

Volunteer Firefighter's Financial Support Program offered payments up to $6,000 for self-employed firefighters. The list went on. Grants, payments, support.

Hats off also to the incredible huge-hearted people of the

world. YOU. Those who dipped into pockets and bank accounts, who created ways to give, selflessly sowing into strangers. Those who thought more about others than themselves—and just gave, above and beyond; abundantly! And boy did people give. Incredible! At the time of writing this YOU, you amazing humans who have brought hope to so many, have donated a whopping $170 million.

Thank you!

With tears spilling down my cheeks, I want to send a shout-out to those who risked life and limb to stay with friends and neighbours as they battled to save their homes and properties. Many of these people were not expected, and certainly not trained, to do what they did, but they did it anyway. Throughout history we have recognised a handful of great people who have given their all to help and save others, but who knows that the vast majority will never receive a mention, let alone commendations and medals, for their sacrificial service. On behalf of all of us, I salute you beautiful people. The courage you displayed in our time of need infuses us with strength and gives us a hope for the future.

And thank you to all the volunteers and willing workers who served the needs of others, even though they themselves were undoubtedly fighting their own battles in such trying circumstances. Many acts of service occurred behind the scenes through the coordination of rescue efforts. This includes people such as:

Member for Bega, Andrew Constance MP, who has been hands-on at almost every event, cheering us on, battling for companies and government to open purses and help our communities rise, truly moved by our human suffering.

Eurobodalla Mayor Liz Innes who fought to save her own home in the blackest of nights and has given more than her community could ever have expected—willingly and tirelessly.

Batemans Bay RFS Captain Ian Aitken who possibly ran on a few hours' sleep a day to continue to coordinate round-the-clock teams—constantly fighting for the safety of our communities and not giving up until the last flame was extinguished.

To the many other emergency workers not already mentioned—including ambos, town firies, electrical linesman, hospital staff, psychologists and counsellors; to those quietly running around doing what they could to help ease other people's fear and anxiety. We all say a huge thank you—you are true champions—every last one of you!

Eurobodalla Mayor Liz Innes

Council certainly underwent some challenges, but rose to every occasion. Behind the scenes things were being organised at a frantic pace. Essential Energy worked tirelessly over many hours to get power back on to the Batemans Bay CBD a week earlier than anyone had thought possible. Council workers ran around and physically opened valves that were down because water was being used faster than it could be pumped.

Because Council closes over the Christmas period, people were phoning the offices and only receiving the answering machine. Little did they know that most of the staff, even those who had been on leave, were volunteering from evacuation centres, the fire control office and other places. I was so proud of the crews serving behind the scenes that many people wouldn't even be aware of.

During the crisis, the lead agency was the RFS—all other agencies including National Parks, Forestry and Council were under them. All information went through the RFS and then council fulfilled its role in making sure toilets were flushing, water was getting through and roads were closed and cleared. The difficulty was having all communication lines down. We had radio and that was it, so we weren't always aware of what was happening, or where. It didn't hold anyone back though, it was next level, with us functioning in high-gear together, an interagency group working around the clock!

The fact that we didn't lose hundreds of lives is a credit

to our community listening to warnings, being prepared and supporting each other. Many of us had been preparing our properties months in advance, knowing there weren't enough trucks to cater for this area if things got out of hand.

Our community had two options. One was to get out in advance—to make informed, sensible decisions before the fire hit. The other was to prepare properties, to make them as defendable as they could be. I began months ago. I started with my main house and worked my way out, moving combustible materials as far away from the main house as possible. I had one large paddock for the horses, with the gates open. Then I worked from the little house. In preparedness I had my saddles and camping gear in the horse float and had raked leaves. We wet hessian bags and placed them around doorframes. The gutters were blocked, we had pumps from the river and firefighting hoses from a truck with a tank of water on it. I knew we'd be staying to defend our house when the fire hit. We did our research, as we encouraged everyone to do.

I knew there was a monster sitting out there, I wanted my place as safe as it possibly could be.

A friend was camped by the river and woke us up around 2.30am to tell us the fire was getting bigger and louder—it was coming. We had a cup of tea and everyone enacted our fire plan—my 11-year-old daughter Ivy did everything right. Together we fought that monster from about 2.30am to 6am when it swept over us and went to Mogo and beyond.

'This is okay, we've got this,' I was thinking. We all just did our thing. We fought with all that we had. We watched it take our big shed, turning it into rubble. We couldn't believe it when it finally went over us—we had saved our house and we were all alive. It had come from the ridge to the west and went straight over the top of us. For a time I didn't know if the horses were dead or alive. Fortunately they survived, exhausted but all okay.

At 6.45am we all sat down and had a cold beer, watching the flames in the trees all around us. Then at 7.30am we saw the other fire heading into town toward the back of the industrial estate. We watched it head in to wipe out parts of Batemans Bay. I phoned as many as I could get in contact with. I knew our neighbour round from me was in a gully in a timber house. I wanted to know what had happened for 80-year-old Bob. The Nelligen boys, worried for his life, cut their way in toward his house and found a note: 'Saved house. Am okay. Bob' written on a piece of cardboard with black coal. As soon as they touched the note, it fell apart.

It took my partner Spike seven hours to cut his way out of our property. We needed to get Ivy to Mum's. My daughter had an extra burden to carry during this time because she had to share her Mum with the town. As Mayor, I had a lot to deal with and wanted to do it well. Through everything I found the hardest was hardly seeing Ivy. I saw her for only a few hours in those first five days because I was dedicating myself to my community at the evacuation centre and across the Shire where I was needed.

Through this whole experience, capturing stories is crucial. It brings understanding and healing. It helps us, in each telling, to not get stuck in the trauma but to be able to look away, look to the future.

I plead with everyone to listen to warnings, prepare your home and know your fire plan. We have to have the conversations. We live in a hot, dry country, preparedness is the key. We need to learn from this; we can't have things like this fire, repeating itself.

We have to do more slashing, more hazard reduction. It is time to address the fire code. We need to consider whether bunkers are a reality for those in remote areas. The community need to attend open days at the RFS and learn how to be fire-prepared. We live in tricky times. The biggest threat to ourselves is our complacency.

Now, more than ever, my goal is to assist in leading people out of the trauma, that's what my leadership is all about.

Liz's daughter, Ivy

I knew our fire plan. I wanted to stay home and help my parents defend our house. We had been preparing it for months, so I knew we were safe. We'd gone over the plan and I was ready—I had boots, jeans and my grandpa's cotton shirt that Mum says has got his angel wings attached to it. I had a wet blanket. I stayed up late and it seemed that 20 minutes after I went to sleep, Mum was waking me up. I got changed and grabbed the bag that I really wanted. That was the one bag I needed and wanted to save. It wasn't long after 2.30am and I got up and went outside and fought for the house. I saw the shed go up. I stayed low until the front went over.

It was the most exciting Christmas I've ever had. One of my favourite bits was after the fire passed and the sky was orange. We were all sitting relaxing by then, eating stuff. It felt good.

RFS Captain Ian Aitken

It is important that what happened has been documented. Our community came together as one, stronger than ever before. People helping people—conscious now of what really matters. It is great to be given this opportunity to share our story.

And then there are those close to me, family and friends. As I think about my friends and how supportive it was to be in contact with them through the crazy days and through the calm—I am so glad we had set-up our Friend's page on Messenger. None of us realised how valuable it would become.

Feeling isolated and lonely during these trying times is not something any of us would want to contemplate. It's amazing how important, and therapeutic, it has been, and is, to share our thoughts and feelings with one another. Having contact with the girls took the edge off fear and it lessened the emotional pain we all inevitably carried. Our survival and recovery may even depend on that sense of being a part of a whole, more than we tend to realise.

Through most of what we have just been through, I wasn't really concerned for me and Step (that's the least of it really, as we always seem to bounce back), but I had Mum with me, I had my children and grandchildren all around—all facing their own challenges, and all trying to deal with their own fears. Knowing my girlfriends had my back in prayer was a big relief. It also provided us girls with an inner strength and peace that we may not otherwise have had.

As the first week of February rolled passed, even after our year's hottest Batemans Bay temperature on February 1 at 43.2°C, it seemed that everyone was busy adjusting. With the heat and the flames, we were all reeling as though we'd been run over by a truck. How do you get up and try to find some sort of order? I asked the girls how they were doing.

Susan, always the gracious one

I just felt that my peace and confidence in God was a gift. Nothing to do with rewarding my faith. Common sense was still with me however, and I knew I would have been a hindrance to my son and a super stress on my youngest son if I hadn't evacuated. I just spent my time talking to people and reassuring them and encouraging those who had lost their homes. Now I'm going through 'survivor guilt' as I hear people's stories. And crying a lot.

Sylvia, deep, raw and real

At the time of the fires at the evacuation centre, I felt abandoned and helpless. For me, I couldn't just focus on myself, I had my grandkids and Jodie to think of. In an out-of-control situation, most of the time I just tried to hold myself together. And my fear wasn't about death or losing stuff, it was about keeping my family safe. And I felt inadequate. In spite of it all, I find my strength in God, and upon reflection, I ask myself, why I was so fearful about my family? I know they're in good hands and that's what saw my strength and comfort return.

Robin, strong and mighty

I was calm most of the time during the past seven weeks. Just once when the fire turned back on our street I was a bit scared and thought I may have to 'get out of here.' But the situation quickly eased and I could see I was safe. I was constantly relying on God to tell me when and if I should leave.

I reckon I used my common sense pretty well in assessing the risk to me and my property but I could have been more organised about evacuating if I needed to. I think I felt safer here than anywhere else. I needed God's presence most when the wind changed and the fire came back toward us again. His presence was with me all the time. I couldn't have done it without trusting Him. He had never failed me before and I knew He wasn't about to leave me when I needed Him so urgently. He is faithful and I knew He'd be with me all the way, *'a very present help in the time of trouble'*.

The day before the fire came almost to my door, God spoke to me, 'I am walking beside you.' All through the worst day of the fire, I remembered those words. I remained calm and was able to calm others through my trusting God. Since then, the love and hugs of my sisters has soothed the raw remembrance of the day.

Before the rain

It was the day before any rain had come. Hot, dry, smoky, difficult and beautiful. The date was Thursday February 6, 2020.

Yesterday I burst into tears three times.

Yesterday I laughed out loud with friends.

Yesterday I ran a group for women being raw and real.

Yesterday I stood alone beside the rubble that is my daughter's home after the fires.

Yesterday I shared gluten-free steak sandwiches with some beautiful friends.

Yesterday I celebrated the reprinting of my first book.

Yesterday I heard that my children's book is heading to me in the mail to approve.

Yesterday I sat on the floor with my daughter sorting through bags and bags of donated clothes for her and her children.

Yesterday I met a new puppy.

Yesterday I listened to an inspirational podcast from Southland.

Yesterday I hugged my hubby.

Yesterday I checked on a friend still surviving life in a fire zone.

Yesterday I listened as Step shared his day over dinner.

Yesterday I wrote some more on my new book. (Postscript: you're holding it now)

Yesterday I did some Brain Gym with my six-year-old grandson to help settle him.

Yesterday I walked the beach.

Yesterday I prayed.

Yesterday I loved.

Every day is filled with so many little things. Good and bad, side-by-side as I navigate life and choose where I'll fix my focus. For me, it is about being present, soaking it in, really loving it.

I wrote 'Yesterday I' the day after I visited my daughter's

burnt-down home. I had gone on my own to her block of land, their broken home still a puddled mess of tin and brick on blackened earth, surrounded by burnt and fallen trees. In my heart, I knew I was to go back there. It had been a month since I last confronted 'the elephant in the room' and felt I needed the visit, if only to help process my own feelings. During my time there, I thought I handled it well, yet just hours later when Susan asked me how I went, I broke down in tears. It was a strange, emotional day.

And in it all, this challenge came to me. Join me if you dare. Let's now look around our homes. Take in all of our beautiful things, every last one of them—pictures and lounges and photos and furnishings. Then let's close our eyes and leave them closed until all we have behind our eyelids is blackness... and the memory of all those possessions we were just appreciating. The only difference between us and those who lost everything, is that we get to open our eyes—and everything is still there!

I believe those who lost everything will recover and will receive more than they had before. I actually prophesy this over them all. Amanda, my beautiful friend who lost everything, told me yesterday that she has noticed a shift—a lift. She'd had a dream where she opened the drawer in her old kitchen and it was full of utensils bulging out of it, so much so that she needed to search through each time she wanted something. When she awoke from her dream, she was so glad that was no longer the case. Her life has been streamlined. It hurt. It hurt like crazy, and will continue to do so off and on for a long time. But right now, she is able to see good shining out. She doesn't live in clutter; she's been given an opportunity to start again. And she is so grateful for all the new things she has and will be able to have again because she lives in such a beautiful world, where people care about others, where sharing and giving are a first-response, where kindness is helping her rebuild her life.

And then the rain

And would you believe, after months and months of drought and fire, the rains came. On February 7, 2020, we got rain! The next morning, I rose before dawn, energised by the new day. I greeted the natives that met me outside with a wave— kangaroos munching on the grass, a kookaburra who just happened to swoop down as I walked out the door, tiny blue wrens and finches under the palms; the ducks swimming on the dam and the eastern water dragons lazing on logs, awaiting the sun to get them going.

It had rained. Unbelievable! I could not remember how long it had it been since water actually fell from the sky! Who knows? Months? Way too many months. I breathe in the rain and smile at the wonder of it all. How quickly life can change.

The driest day of 2020 was recorded on January 10 with 0.0 millimetres of rain or condensation.

The wettest day of 2020 was recorded only a month later on February 10 with 140.2 millimetres of rain falling.

Before these rains that burst like a flood upon us, it was not just difficult, but almost impossible to comprehend just how much had been destroyed of this once pristine coastal region, with our once beautiful, relaxing, bushy drives. Even if (it was too hard to say 'when'), yes, even if we get the fires under control, even when the fires finally cease and are history, it won't be over. Rain won't magically put an end to our struggle. The struggle continues. Will there be an end? Will it take until 2022 before our homes are rebuilt and our town's economies are restored? Who knows?

Will the rains wash away what stands before our community now? No. We are the homeless and the jobless, we are small businesses struggling to stay afloat, we are a township of people who've gone without regular income for a long time. The repercussions for our tourist-dependent towns after being denied the summer's earnings is huge. Along with our material recovery, we have the physical as well as the mental/emotional recovery to deal with. Just today I heard of two small shops closing down.

We need energy. We need courage. We need strength. We need hope. We need God.

And here I am now, damp grass under my barefoot toes; a flock of white cockatoos creating a ruckus in one of the tall trees on a fresh and lively morning. I release a prayer of gratitude. I might walk through the bush with my boots on, or I might don my cossies and do laps in the pool. Either way, I will move my body, maybe even dance in it!

I dance in it. *Kisses* pouring from Heaven. It is raining! I'll let Sylvia sum it up, 'Well, here's the rain, a blessing from God. Washing away a layer of soot and dust. Settling things and then making things grow again, renewing and revitalising us!'

Some of the fresh new plants have exploded from seed pods that only fire could bring to life. Other black trunks are now covered in bright green leaves. Could things finally be looking up?

The National Bushfire Recovery Agency (NBRA) has asked people to respond with cash instead of clothing and food. We had so much donated that St Vincent De Paul and Salvation Army stores had more than they could cope with and announced they couldn't take any more. The NBRA said:

> To help services deal effectively and efficiently with the ongoing recovery the Government is asking that donations be in the form of financial assistance only. The response has been so great, coordination services are struggling to manage the volume of goods and materials coming in.

Of course, just like the looters that were stealing from homes that had been evacuated, and even helping themselves to the few possessions people were able to take to the evacuation centres, there were scammers online. The NBRA announced, 'Of the wide range of appeals raising funds for people and animals affected by the bushfires, some of these are scams.' Our friends from Lake Conjola who lost their home, were alerted to a fundraising page set up to help them. Complete with their photos and story, this money was being channelled into some hacker's bank account. Though most of our stories are beautiful, you can count on finding a few self-centred opportunists looking to kick people when they're down.

And then on Monday, February 10 there are flash-floods. From fires to floods—roads that have only recently reopened after the fire damage have now been closed due to flood damage. Oh this 'lucky country' of ours. Fire and flood and everything in-between.

Eurobodalla Council and NSW Government release a statement:

> Fire debris washed into waterways from recent heavy rain has resulted in dangerous conditions and poor water quality. Some beaches may have been affected by sewer overflows, and these have been signposted. Many of Eurobodalla's rivers, bays and beaches are covered with burnt twigs and branches, timber, and a fair amount of litter. This is true for the entire southern NSW coastline.... The debris will continue to accumulate but, over time, nature will take its course and Eurobodalla's waterways and 143 kilometres of coastline will be cleansed of organic matter.

At the time of writing this book, the third week of February, the beaches still look like warzones and the colour of the water is just like everything else around us—dirty brown to black.

Yet there's an overwhelming sense that this trauma will eventually turn out to be a good thing, for many of us at least. The fires have changed us, but as we look around, we see green shoots everywhere. Whether its fire or rain, things are always changing. Now is an opportunity for us to make sure the changes we make are the right ones. It is amazing what can grow out of pain. From things dead and black grow the new shoots of life. Tiny shoots to begin, but there's hope in every one. Hope abounds. Let's claim that for our hearts, too.

'It is amazing what can grow out of pain. From things dead and black grow the new shoots of life.'

'*When The Smoke Clears* is our record of the pain and suffering the Australian bushfires brought and the resilience and creativity of those who have travelled though the trauma and of those who continue to gently traverse the long path ahead. With understanding and support, together we will navigate a way forward, ever mindful that the real issues do not go away when the smoke clears.'

CHAPTER 16

I'm so everything at the moment

We are delivered a late Valentine's Day gift when on February 16, 2020, NSW Rural Fire Service officially announce:

> For the first time this season so far, all bush and grass fires in NSW are contained. It has taken a lot of work by firefighters and emergency services as well as communities across the state to get to this point. We still have some time to go before the end of the bush fire season, so it is important that you and your family have a bush fire survival plan and know what you will do in the event a fire threatens.

Seven weeks on, 44 days after the New Year's Eve fires, after 82 continuous days of fire in our shire, though the smoke may have cleared, virtually none of the devastated house-blocks have been. People are still staring at a mountain of debris, facing their loss over and over. It is a state of limbo for some, where feelings are mixed and unstable. Some are angry, others sad. In spite of everything, most feel proud of what the community has achieved together. Some have hit their wall, while others are yet to express their grief and are wondering when their 'big cry' will come.

Some are planning 'big nights out' where talking, laughing and crying together are commonplace, while others 'never want to think about it again'. All face their situation differently, but for many it is with a grieving and aching heart. One friend told me, 'It feels like everyone is just waiting, wondering where to go from here.'

'Knowing in a few months we have to move again is like holding your breath and trying to breathe!'

Amidst the rollercoaster of emotions, some are looking at buying a new home—but houses are selling like hotcakes because the fires have caused a boom in the housing market. Others are struggling with the notion of rebuilding on blocks of land not yet cleared of brokenness. I saw one friend's comment on Facebook which sums up the confusion and emotional struggle many are feeling; 'I'm so *everything* at the moment.'

My daughter Kelita can so relate to that statement right now. She said there's a sense of dysfunction, that feeling of, 'I don't fit anywhere now.'

Kelita

I've always been one who loves change. I thought change was my thing, but when it was forced upon me, I wasn't ready for it, it was hard. Harder than I thought.

Knowing in a few months we have to move again is like holding your breath and trying to breathe!

Like so many others who have lost their homes, we're in a constant phase of uncertainty. It's a process and I'm trying to go with it, but always in the back of my mind is how many steps there are to move forward.

We've decided not to rebuild on the old block. There is too much heartache and pain associated with it now. And the views are destroyed; the once thick bush is nothing but blackened tree trunks. So, we are in the position of looking for a home to purchase. It's an interesting experience where hubby and I have this sense of excitement as we drive to view each home the real estate agents direct us to. On the way, we feel 'up', with a 'could this be it?' thrill attached to it, and then the crash of disappointment when each home isn't right for us. And though we don't want to be down, our minds go there anyway. It is as if depression hits us like a brick to the head.

It's not so much stress, where we're worried about things, it is more anxiety—where we're not quite in control of our lives. We're unsettled and no sense of peace or ease comes to relieve that. And well, we just don't feel happy.

At the end of the day, I'm just doing what I always do... getting the kids off to school, going to work and sharing a meal at night as a family. There's this sense that everyone else thinks I look and act the same but I'm wondering, am I acting that way or have I pushed my feelings far enough down to pretend they're not there? I don't even know.

One of the contributing factors to the angst of it all is the fact that everyone we talk to is going through something. There is no break from the fire talk here on the South Coast. Every person, everywhere we turn, is struggling in some way. I can't help but think, 'Just let me stand on top of a mountain away from it all and take in a big breath. That's what I need. I need room to breathe!'

I used to go to the gym, take the kids to the park, have cuppas with friends. Those little things that make life fun. I miss that. I want some of that back in my life. Every second of our days seem to be filled with trying to make this house homier for the kids or looking at houses or checking emails, buying tools or working out where we want to settle later, making sure the insurance claims can be finalised or helping hubby apply for jobs.

According to Clinical Psychologist Dr Rob Gordon, what Kelita and the others who have lost their homes are going through, is 'very normal'. Dr Gordon has been helping communities recover from disasters for more than 35 years and his 'Communities In Disaster'[1] presentation was posted on the Eurobodalla Shire's website as a community resource. We include some of his excellent material here, with permission.

Time and complexity

Some important considerations around any disaster include the length of time it takes to recover, the complexity and variety of factors involved, and the impact disaster has on social processes.

Disasters impact entire communities, not just individuals. They disrupt normal routines which are essential for maintaining normal life and if people are left in this state for too long it can become destructive. It's vital that we don't put all of our efforts into alleviating the physical and material needs of the community without giving due consideration to the social processes involved.

Disaster's inevitable process

The inevitable process associated with disaster looks like this:

1. Pre-disaster—this is the time when routines, social structures, closeness and distance are all in place and everyone has their own unique set of attachments.

2. Impact of disaster—this upsets our normal routines and social connections forcing us into survival mode and what is referred to as 'de-bonding'*.

3. Immediate aftermath—this is when people become disoriented, bewildered or go into a highly excited state.

* *The length of time in this de-bonded state is a strong predictor of psychological trauma reactions.*

To re-establish normality, and to facilitate the re-bonding process, we need to adopt a gentle, peaceful approach with those that have been affected. Wherever possible we should aim to have support services on the scene as soon as possible because this helps recovery and minimises the chance of people becoming resentful towards authorities and those offering assistance. We need to begin the process of communication and negotiation with respect for people's privacy and dignity and not order people about or insist they do things a certain way or impose time pressures on them.

In this phase, individuals won't be focused on the long-term repercussions of what has happened and will generally feel euphoric and even happy having survived the disaster, with a sense of 'we're all in this together'. Not long after this, as people are starting to rebuild their lives and re-establish relationships, eruptions of negative emotions like anger and hostility can occur. This is because people have lots of different problems to sort through, with some fully insured and others with no insurance, some directly affected and others only partly affected, but still traumatised nonetheless. Early intervention at this stage helps to prevent cleavages and divisions within the community.

We need to respond with strategies that prioritise all the normal activities that energise people, things like hobbies, leisure activities, enjoyment and intimacy. With so much to do and organise, people tend to forget about these essentials but if we don't address these needs, we can end up with very expensive and sad long-term losses in relationships and family togetherness.

Then comes the community development where we look for constructive growth beyond simply repairing the damage. After a disaster, communities move and change, which can mean new communities with different goals and objectives. Recovery is complete when we are once again leading the life we want to lead and heading towards our chosen life goals.

The final stage involves creating a new identity for the community. This is where leaders need to promote opportunities for people to come together, to tell their stories and reflect on what has happened. It's a time to acknowledge loss, pain and suffering as well as celebrating and recording the resilience and creativity of the community.

Many of those trapped in this unforeseen space, have told me that there doesn't seem an end to it. For some, the short-term chaos keeps clouding the long-term vision in a different kind of smokescreen—an emotional fog. Others say nothing seems linear about arriving at a specific destination, there are just too many variables, too many people, tradies, insurance claims, timelines and red-tape to navigate.

My youngest daughter Jordan concludes:

> Now is the time for this book to come out. I believe it is so timely. Just when everyone is feeling like we've all been forgotten and the world has moved on from caring about the South Coast, these raw stories, reminders of faith and community… a glimmer of hope… bring the focus back where it needs to go.

I would add now is a time for those outside our devastated communities to come in and spend money, bring joy and stimulate our local economies, offering hope for our future. It is a time to remind ourselves not to grow tired in doing good.[2]

Now is a daunting time for so many. It isn't just the smoke and the fires and the loss of homes and the destruction everywhere and the animals that have perished and the lives that were lost and the grief we continue to struggle to process; it is the reality that people's lives have been completely turned upside down so that their futures are now a tangle of unpredictable twists and turns. Recovery is a challenging pathway that may include psychological first aid, rethinking priorities, new jobs, changing addresses, kids changing schools, the unfamiliarity of new neighbourhoods, or waiting months—possibly years—to move back into a new home at the old address.

Nevertheless, now is also a time when our communities remember what's really important. It is a time for all of us to pull together, to be positive, to lean on one another, to share love and to celebrate each small victory.

When The Smoke Clears is our record of the pain and suffering the Australian bushfires brought and the resilience and creativity of those who have travelled though the trauma and of those who continue to gently traverse the long path ahead. With understanding and support, together we will navigate a way forward, ever mindful that the real issues do not go away when the smoke clears.

[1] Dr Rob Gordon has spent the past 35 years working with people affected by emergencies and disasters. Rob was there in the aftermath of the Bali bombings and Christchurch earthquake, Black Saturday, the Canberra firestorm, the Tasmanian bushfires, as well as many other large-scale disasters — and most recently the 2019 Australian bushfire emergency. He has advised the Red Cross and governments on how to assist individual people and whole communities as they rebuild and recover. Here is just one example of his assistance: https://youtu.be/SBvJw3nBqKg

[2] This advice is subject to Covid-19 restrictions and guidelines which have come quickly after the fires. Please see the Postscript to this book for more information.

'Covid-19 and the pandemic response has certainly turned our world upside down, and yet only three months ago many communities such as on the NSW South Coast already had their lives turned upside down and inside out.'

POSTSCRIPT

Covid 19

When I finished writing this book in February 2020, the NSW South Coast and other parts of Australia ravaged by bushfire, were only just starting along the road to recovery. Even then, the first glimpses of another menace had begun to appear on the horizon. A new strain of coronavirus, later designated Covid-19, was beginning to impact nations around the world.

Ironically, China first notified the World Health Organisation (WHO) of a spate of unexplained pneumonia cases in Wuhan City, Hubei province, on December 31, 2019, the very same day that out-of-control bushfires raged violently through the Eurobodalla region and beyond, changing our lives forever.

Fast-forward to early April and as the Covid-19 pandemic continues to dominate media headlines, spreading its contagion of fear and uncertainty across the globe, it appears that Australia and the world have all but forgotten the bushfire tragedy and the multitudes who are no closer to rebuilding their homes or putting the pieces of their shattered lives back together.

Having earlier issued a hopeful call for tourists to return to our beautiful but burnt region, we are now asking people not to come as our limited health resources could not cope if there was an outbreak here.

It has been heartening to hear someone remembering our plight, none less than retiring RFS Chief Shane Fitzsimmons who will now head a new NSW Government agency, Resilience NSW. On the morning his appointment was announced (April 6, 2020), he made a point of talking ɔout the victims of bushfire, almost as a counterpoint to the constant stream of Covid-19 news:

> There was never a more important time to make sure that communities devastated by drought, bushfires and now Covid-19 are getting the help they need to rebuild and recover. How heartbreaking was it last week when the Deputy Premier issued the press release to request people stay away from rural and regional NSW. The last couple of months we have desperately wanted people out there to help rebuild, to help them spend money. We're really keen as a state in NSW to get our planning instruments and prevention instruments in place, and most importantly get that recovery underway, straight away. I am very keen to play a role in that space and I'm optimistic that I can make a difference working with an extraordinary team of people to help those who have been so terribly affected by the disasters they have experienced.

There is no doubt that resilience is what we desperately need, and so I welcome Mr Fitzsimmons optimism as much as I have had cause to welcome a miraculous change of wind, turning away a firestorm.

The fact remains that the world is in crisis and desperately searching for a way forward. Covid-19 and the pandemic response has certainly turned our world upside down, and yet only three months ago many communities such as on the NSW South Coast already had their lives turned upside down and inside out.

While it is understandable that people are panicked and living from day to day, with little thought for what happened three days ago let alone three months ago, we should be mindful of all those poor souls who were promised so much assistance, only to have the teams of volunteers, clean-up crews and tradies vanish before any real progress was achieved.

The concern is that thousands of people who are still suffering and struggling to cope may be forgotten and left to fend for themselves without the essential support they need from government and their fellow Australians.

It is my prayer that this book, *When The Smoke Clears*, not only gives voice to those who directly endured Australia's worst-ever bushfire season, but acts as a reminder as we wait for another disaster to pass, that we are here, that we need you, that we could be you....

It's not my style to let the heaviness of these circumstances be the final word, especially when every day I'm touched by the beauty and wonder I see re-emerging, kisses from heaven of course, if you know me at all. And so I return once again to the word that is the final word:

Whoever dwells in the shelter of the Most High will rest in the shadow of the Almighty. I will say of the Lord, 'He is my refuge and my fortress, my God, in whom I trust.' Psalm 91:1,2 (NIV)

Acknowledgements

No matter how many solitary hours a writer sits at her laptop, clicking away under the moonlight into the wee hours of the morning, no book is written alone. The coming together of this story could not have been achieved without the love, support, contribution, encouragement and hard yards of many, many people. Though there are far too many to mention individually, you're too important to not mention at all.

This book is for all who have known grief, who have struggled and to those who have discovered the healing power of reaching out to others upon your journey. You matter!

A special thank you brimming with love must go to those dearest to my heart—Step Guinery (my lover, my world); that wild bunch that make up this zany family—Ben Guinery, Lauren Edwards and darling River; Garren, Cassia, Ella and Mia Walton; Kelita and clan; Caleb, Tess, Peaches, Hopps and Junee Guinery; Mace, Jordan, Willow, Chili, Hayz, Oaky and Cove Innes and my extraordinary mother Janice Aitken.

To the friends who journey alongside me—Susan Poke, Robin Malcolm, Sylvia Scanlan, Elsie Radburn and Pam Buddle; and bestie Elaine Rogers. To those within the community who went above and beyond—Gonz and Kellie Whittington and girls; Matt Kastelein and the Central Coast community; Wayne and Alison Tarrant and the Campbelltown community; Norm and Sue Fraser; the generous Aitchison clan, thanks for the whole nine yards—and more!

To Kelita and your clan, Amanda Scully, Paula, Scott and Amber, Max and Jody, Mat and Julie Steedman, Jim Hughes, Katrina Condie and to James—may your spirits stay sweet as you rise and conquer.

To the multitude of rescue workers here and everywhere—BlazeAid, Samaritan's Purse, local volunteer organisations such as Red Cross, Vinnies, Anglicare, emptyhouses.org, service clubs and the many more—those who wear uniforms, those who serve our communities, those who shine the light needed when others are going through their deepest darkness; Fire Captain Ian Aitken and Connie, Eurobodalla Mayor Liz Innes, Dr Rob Gordon, Pastors Garren and Cassia Walton —we wouldn't be where we are without you.

To the businesses that continuously served up my almond brewed chai teas—Mark and Kylie at Tribe Café, Grumpy and Sweethearts, JJs on the Marina and the Mossy Café; to Perry Street Cinema; to Innes Boatshed—thank you, and I'll be back!

To our treasured Southland ever-expanding 'family'; brothers Ray and David, and sisters Linda, Karen and Vicki; Aunty Dee, 'counsellor' Donna Hunter; buddies Graeme Jolly and James Paull; Jenny Phillips; Norm and Sue Fraser; Trish Silling; Angela and Alexandra; Isaac Chicco; Helen, Lawrie and family; Sarah Borrowman and Lauren Barlow; Cameron; Kim; Kathie Blankley and Kay Grainger. To ACTS Global Leadership Team Wayne and Ruth Swift; Alex Irvine; the incredibly talented friend and mentor Peter Hallett at Fifty Days Press—nothing, yep nothing, beats a team like this!

And the rest of you: all of you… those who fed, housed, inspired, financed, sowed into, provided shelter, clothing and encouragement, fundraised and gave without holding back—we continue because of you. And the many Facebook, Instagram and Messenger friends who add inspiration at the touch of a button—may you feel my arms of love in a massive virtual hug filled with gratitude.

And to everyone going through their own crisis, experiencing trauma or facing your own battles, yes, this book is dedicated to you.

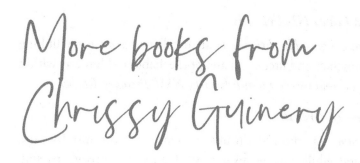

More books from
Chrissy Guinery

Adult

Falling Up Stairs
Room to Breathe

Children's books

Meet Mr Mouse, co-written with 10 year-old Willow Innes, illustrated by 7 year-old Chili Innes

Buzz Loves His Friends, illustrated by 9 year-old Mia Walton

What people are saying

Chrissy's words come from the heart and make me proud to be different. *Nathel*

Falling Up Stairs

Falling Up Stairs is more than a book—it is an event to be thoroughly, absurdly enjoyed—and definitely to be given as gifts for everyone on your Christmas list. You will laugh out loud and you will cry. You will be motivated and inspired and you won't be the same after the journey! *Elaine Rogers, NSW Royal Agricultural Society Events Coordinator*

Buzz Loves His Friends

Buzz Loves His Friends is an excellent resource for linking numeracy and literacy in an approachable and fun way within the classroom. *Lauren Edwards, NSW Primary Teacher*

Room To Breath

Room To Breathe creates a sense of community and hope while raising awareness. I admire Chrissy's passion to help others in this helpful and motivational book. *The Hon Tanya Davies MP, NSW Minister for Mental Health*

What people are saying about *When The Smoke Clears*

Such a raw and real read. Thank you Chrissy and everyone whose stories are represented here. *When The Smoke Clears* is definitely part of our collective healing. *Angela Stewart, Counsellor*

As someone who also experienced the trauma of the bushfires, *When The Smoke Clears* reminds me why it is so important to support each other so we can heal and go forward. It is such an inspiring book! *Barbara Pitkin*

Another inspiring book from Chrissy Guinery. In spite of all we went through, *When The Smoke Clears* shows how kindness, love and compassion came together to override our horrible circumstances. Having lost my own house in Catalina, my heart goes out to all of us. This book helps us continue on the path as we rise up and rebuild our lives. *Judith Ray*

Many tears are shed as I relate to every page of *When The Smoke Clears*. And now I have my very own word to share, for the grief and gratitude—I call it 'griefitude'. It really helps to define the confusion I experience with my many feelings. *Sue Novak*